themes for early years

SCHOLASTIC

C000151015

Myself

Fully revised with CD-ROM

Licence for CD-ROM

IMPORTANT – PERMITTED USE AND WARNINGS – READ CAREFULLY BEFORE INSTALLING

Copyright in the software contained in this CD-ROM and in its accompanying material belongs to Scholastic Limited. All rights reserved. © Scholastic Ltd, 2006.

The material contained on this CD-ROM may only be used in the context for which it was intended in *Themes for Early Years: Myself*. School site use is permitted only within the school of the purchaser of the book and CD-ROM. Permission to download images is given for purchasers only and not for borrowers from any lending service. Any further use of the material contravenes Scholastic Ltd's copyright and that of other rights holders.

Save for these purposes, or as expressly authorised in the accompanying materials, the software may not be copied, reproduced, used, sold, licensed, transferred, exchanged, hired, or exported in whole or in part or in any manner or form without the prior written consent of Scholastic Ltd. Any such unauthorised use or activities are prohibited and may give rise to civil liabilities and criminal prosecutions.

This CD-ROM has been tested for viruses at all stages of its production. However, we recommend that you run virus-checking software on your computer systems at all times. Scholastic Ltd cannot accept any responsibility for any loss, disruption or damage to your data or your computer system that may occur as a result of using either the CD-ROM or the data held on it.

IF YOU ACCEPT THE ABOVE CONDITIONS YOU MAY PROCEED TO USE THIS CD-ROM

Includes Adobe® Reader®

Adobe, the Adobe logo, and Reader are either registered trademarks or trademarks of Adobe Systems Incorporated in the United States and/or other countries.

To enable the running of the videos on the CD-ROM please download the latest version of Apple QuickTime from http://www.apple.com/quicktime/download/win.html

For all technical support queries, please phone Scholastic Customer Services on 0845 603 9091.

To use the activities on the CD included with this book, you will need the following:
● PC with CD and 128 Mb RAM with Microsoft Windows 98SE or higher
● Mac G3 with CD and 128 Mb RAM with System 9.2 or later (Mac OSX classic model only)
● Facilities for printing and sound
● SVGA screen displaying at least 64K colours at a screen size of 800 × 600 pixels.

Jean Evans and Lynne Burgess

themes for early years

Credits

Original material © 1995, Lynne Burgess
Revised material © 2006, Jean Evans
and Lynne Burgess
New material © 2006, Jean Evans
© 2006 Scholastic Ltd

Published by Scholastic Ltd, Book End,
Range Road, Oxfordshire, OX29 0YD

Printed by Bell & Bain Ltd, Glasgow

5 6 7 8 9 0   0 1 2 3 4 5

British Library Cataloguing-in-Publication
Data A catalogue record for this book is
available from the British Library.

ISBN 0-439-96557-8
ISBN 978-0439-96557-6

Visit our website at www.scholastic.co.uk

CD-ROM developed in association with Footmark
Media Ltd

All songs and rhymes performed by Sally Scott and
Simon Anderson.

Authors
Jean Evans and Lynne Burgess

Editor
Jane Bishop

Assistant Editor
Rachel Mackinnon

Series Designers
Joy Monkhouse, Anna Oliwa, Andrea
Lewis and Catherine Mason.

Designers
Allison Parry and Geraldine Reidy

Illustrations
Rebecca Elliott, The Bright Agency

Cover artwork
Maria Maddox

Mixed Sources
Product group from well-managed
forests and other controlled sources
www.fsc.org Cert no. TT-COC-002769
© 1996 Forest Stewardship Council

Acknowledgements

Extracts from *Themes for Early Years: Myself* by Lynne Burgess (1995, Scholastic Limited):
Clive and Thomas Barnwell for the use of 'Shoe choose tune' by Clive and Thomas
Barnwell © 1995, Clive and Thomas Barnwell. **Pie Corbett** for the use of 'Quiet as mice' and
'Animal sounds we can make' by Pie Corbett © 1995, Pie Corbett. **Carole Henderson-Begg** for the
use of 'I'm alive shanty' by Ian Henderson-Begg © 1995, Ian Henderson-Begg. **Rozalia Makinson**
for the use of 'I can' by Rozalia Makinson © 1995, Rozalia Makinson. **Peter Morrell** for the use of
'That hat!' by Peter Morrell © 1995, Peter Morrell.
   Trevor Harvey for the use of 'Bedtime in summer' by Trevor Harvey from *Poetry Corner*
© 1992, Trevor Harvey (1992, BBC Publications). **Sally Scott** for the use of 'Once I was a baby',
'Jump for joy', 'Pets', 'Stop by the road', 'Happy news, sad news', 'Daily routines', 'Best of friends',
'Hand washing', 'Keeping safe', 'Dressing up', 'That's my face', 'Patterns in socks', 'Clapping
clothes', 'Happy helpers', 'All about me', 'This day is a special day', 'Visitors', 'With my hands' and
'My worries' by Sally Scott © 2006, Sally Scott, previously unpublished.

Every effort has been made to trace copyright holders and the publishers apologise for any
omissions.

Contents

Introduction   5

Planner   7

Assessment   8

What do I look like?   9

All about me	9
My body	10
PCP Head, shoulders, knees and toes	11
Mirror activities	12
PCP Mirror images	13
Self-portraits	14
Welcome albums	15
Matching bodies	16
PCP Tops and bottoms	17
Face puzzles	18
PCP Jigsaw faces	19
Baby match	20

What do I wear?   21

Dressing up	21
What's in the bag?	22
PCP Find the pairs	23
Clapping clothes	24
Shoe mimes	25
Socks on the washing line	26
PCP Hang them out	27
Hat game	28
PCP Match the hats	29
Baby clothes	30
Birthday badge	31

Who shares my home?   32

Family portraits	32
Family treasure hunt	33
Pets	34
PCP The pet shop	35
Crossing safely	36
PCP Safely home	37
Dressing a doll family	38
PCP Match the clothes	39
Dangers at home	40
PCP Keeping safe	41
Birthdays	42
Visitors	43

What can I do?   44

Helping	44
PCP Happy helpers	45
Experimenting with beanbags	46
PCP Beanbags	47
What I can do	48
My hands	49
Mark-making challenge	50
Working together	51
Our day	52
PCP My day	53
Body sounds	54

themes for early years

How do I feel? 55

Worry tree	55
Happy and sad news	56
The happiest day of my life	57
Things that scare me	58
PCP Little Miss Muffet	59
Friendship	60
PCP Friendship bracelets	61
Happy and sad music	62
Good moods	63
Jump for joy	64

How can I look after myself? 65

Wash your hands	65
Eat more fruit	66
PCP Draw and count	67
Skeletons	68
Hoop game	69
Milkshake	70
PCP Apricot milkshakes	71
Go to sleep	72
Road safety	73
Time lines	74

Displays 75

Body parts	75
Shoe prints	76
Action words	77
Daily routines	78

Songs 79

I'm alive shanty	79
With my hands	79
That hat!	80
Shoe choose tune	80
All about me	81
Pets	82
Visitors	83
Jump for joy	84
Stop by the road	85
This day is a special day	86

Rhymes 87

Tommy Thumb	87
Quiet as mice	87
I can	88
Animal sounds we make	89
Bedtime in summer	89
That's my face	90
Dressing up	90
Once I was a baby	91
My worries	91
Clapping clothes	92
Happy helpers	92
Hand washing	93
Best of friends	93
Patterns in socks	94
Happy news, sad news	94
Daily routines	95
Keeping safe	95

CD-ROM
- All songs sung with musical accompaniment
- All songs music-only version
- All rhymes spoken
- 18 photocopiable pages
- Ten full-colour photographs
- Five on-screen activities
- Three film clips

Introduction

Using themes in early years

A well-chosen theme should include activities planned to ensure that each child can contribute from firsthand experience and interest, and that previous knowledge can be further enhanced. As children take part they should be given time to explore aspects of the theme independently, with appropriate adult support, and develop their own ideas as they play.

Many early years practitioners plan cross-curricular topics because of the advantages offered by an integrated approach. Young children naturally make links across the curriculum. They are not constrained by thinking of learning within distinct areas; they learn holistically through play.

As with the planning of all activities, particularly those involving food preparation, it is essential to check for any allergies or dietary requirements that children might have before they take part.

The theme 'Myself'

'Myself' provides an excellent initial topic for children first encountering a new educational setting and, as such, is one of the most popular early years topics. Young children are often self-centred and eager to talk about themselves, and communication at this level enables adults to get to know them. It also helps children to find out more about each other.

How to use this book

All activities in the book link to the *Curriculum guidance for the foundation stage* (QCA), with a good balance of Early Learning Goals and Stepping Stones across the six Areas of Learning.

Six chapters in the book cover common aspects of self-discovery such as physical appearance (Chapters 1 and 2), family (Chapter 3), achievements (Chapter 4), emotions (Chapter 5) and health education (Chapter 6). Assessment is included with brief

comments explaining how observing children's actions and listening to their vocabulary as they take part in an activity can provide valuable evidence for assessment for each activity. This assessment can then provide the basis for future planning to meet the needs of individuals.

The final chapter in the book suggests ideas for setting up stimulus displays linked to the various themes in this book. Most of the displays are interactive, to encourage the children to become actively involved. Whenever possible, encourage the children to gather and select resources and have them help to assemble the display.

There are ten songs and seventeen rhymes in the book, each linked to an activity idea. The music and lyrics of the songs are included in the book and there are audio versions on the CD-ROM. Spoken versions of the rhymes are also included on the CD-ROM. There are 18 photocopiable activity sheets, each linked with a specific activity idea in the book. Printable versions of these sheets are also included on the CD-ROM.

What's on the CD-ROM

The CD-ROM that accompanies this book contains valuable resources including photographs, film clips, music and photocopiable sheets. These can be integrated easily into the main activity ideas to extend children's interests and learning.

The photographs – ten attractive images in full colour provide stimulating starting points for discussions related to many of the activity ideas. Children will enjoy looking at them on the computer screen, or printing them off to use in discussions and activities.

The film clips – three film clips involving children playing with a guinea pig, celebrating a birthday and crossing the road provide further opportunity for activity related discussions.

On-screen activities – children love the challenge of computer games and these five simple activities will develop their technology skills whilst extending their participation in the linked activity idea. The activities include: Hang out the washing, Let's make a healthy meal, Little Miss Muffet, Tops and bottoms, and What's in the parcel?

Audio versions of the songs and rhymes – adults will welcome the addition of these lively versions of the songs and rhymes in the book, and children will be able to access them independently using a portable CD-ROM player. There are also music-only versions of the songs.

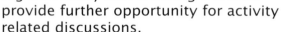
Play again

Match the picture pieces

Printable versions of the photocopiable sheets – this valuable resource will enable adults to print their own activity sheets rather than photocopy those in the book.

Planner

Use this guide to link the activity ideas into your planning for the six Areas of Learning.

Communication, Language and Literacy

All about me	9
Dressing up	21
Pets	34
Crossing safely	36
Visitors	43
What I can do	48
My hands	49
Happy and sad news	56

Personal, Social and Emotional Development

Welcome albums	15
Birthday badge	31
Family portrait	32
Dangers at home	40
Birthdays	42
Working together	51
Worry tree	55
The happiest day of my life	57
Things that scare me	58
Good moods	63

Mathematical Development

Socks on the washing line	26
Baby clothes	30
Family treasure hunt	33
Eat more fruit	66
Milkshake	70
Time lines	74

Myself

Creative Development

My body	10
Self portrait	14
Clapping clothes	24
Mark-making challenge	50
Body sounds	54
Friendship	60
Happy and sad music	62

Physical Development

Face puzzles	18
Shoe mimes	25
Dressing a doll family	38
Experimenting with beanbags	46
Jump for joy	64
Wash your hands	65
Hoop game	69
Go to sleep	72

Knowledge and Understanding of the World

Mirror activities	12
Matching bodies	16
Baby match	20
What's in the bag	22
Hat game	28
Helping	44
Our day	52
Skeletons	68
Road safety	73

Assessment

Brief tips on assessment accompany all the main activity ideas in this book. These suggestions involve observing the children as they are taking part in the activities and listening to what they say. They are usually linked to the learning objectives and designed to support practitioners in likely aspects of development that might be noticeable during the activity.

In addition, skilled awareness of individual children's abilities alongside close observation will often identify progression or difficulties in another learning area.

Above all, it is important to resist the temptation to set up adult-led activities specifically to determine whether a child can manage a particular task.

Spontaneous observation

Spontaneous observation should be recognised as an essential component of your planning and assessment cycle. It is a means of discovering exactly what a child can do and say, and avoids the possibility of assumptions based on what that child is expected to be doing. It is important to watch closely as individual children work and play, rather than concentrate on what they produce as a result of their actions.

Listening

Many of the assessment suggestions focus on listening to the language children use. By noting exactly what is said, whether it be complex vocabulary or first attempts at simple words, it will be possible to reinforce a child's early language development. Resist the temptation to say things for the children and give them time to respond or make comments without interruption.

Spontaneous recording

Have a notebook available to jot down the children's actions and vocabulary at the time they happen, and consider these later before adding relevant comments to your record files. It is essential to have a consistent efficient system in place, which is understood and implemented by all staff, in order to build up a picture of a child's progress over time.

Simple tips for observing and listening

- Give yourself time to focus on an individual or group of children.
- Share the results of your observations with colleagues in order to evaluate a child's progress.
- Try to watch without distracting and listen without interrupting.
- Make sure that your interpretation of a child's understanding of a situation is accurate by asking appropriate questions or discussing problems.
- Observe individuals again in similar situations if specific concerns arise about an aspect of development.

What do I look like?

This chapter explores the different body parts of the children. When you lead children to compare themselves with others, start with similarities rather than differences.

themes for early years

ON THE CD-ROM
Song 'All about me'

All about me

Mark-making

What you need
Name cards; photographs of the children; sugar paper; white and coloured paper; magazines; glue; glue sticks; scissors; felt-tipped pens; stapler.

Preparation
Ask the children to bring in a recent photograph of themselves.

What to do
Sing the 'All about me' song on page 81 and then ask the children if they would like to make a book about themselves to read to their friends. Fold an A3 sheet of sugar paper in half to form the book cover and invite the children to stick their photographs on the front and write their names underneath. Provide name cards and support if necessary.

Discuss what the children would like to include in their books, such as a page about favourite foods, and ask how they might do this, for example, by cutting out pictures of favourite foods from magazines and sticking them onto a page with a caption alongside. Assemble the finished pages inside the cover sheet and staple along the folded edge to form the book.

Discussion
Ask the children to take turns to read their books aloud and ask them questions about the content. These questions will help to inspire descriptive writing. Encourage the children to respect differences by making comparisons between their appearances, and their likes and dislikes.

Follow-up activities
● Display the finished books in the book corner and encourage children to read them individually, in groups or with an adult.
● Add simple information books about families from different cultures to the display.

Differentiation
Instead of making books with younger or less able children create a simple display with drawings and concentrate on describing physical features. Encourage more able children to make books with a specific personal theme.

Sound

themes for early years

STEPPING STONE
Respond to sound with body movement.

EARLY LEARNING GOAL
Recognise and explore how sounds can be changed, sing simple songs from memory, recognise repeated sounds and sound patterns and match movements to music. (CD)

ASSESSMENT
Observe individual children taking part in the song. How well do they link their movements to the words? Do they understand the vocabulary?

My body

What you need
The song 'Head, shoulders, knees and toes' from *Okki-Tokki-Unga* (A & C Black).

What to do
Share the song with the children, asking them to touch each body part as it is named. When they are familiar with this, ask them to point to the body parts of a friend while singing.

Demonstrate the idea of substituting silence for each word in turn by miming touching each body part. Begin by missing out the word 'heads' when it is mentioned, and continue to repeat the song, missing out another body part, until the entire song is being mimed.

Discussion
Encourage the children to sing together, pointing to their body parts at the same time. Talk about the different types of movement each body part can make, and challenge the children to demonstrate various ways of moving their heads or shoulders. Emphasise the need for children to sing the missing words silently to themselves in order to follow the song.

Follow-up activities
● Provide each child with a copy of the photocopiable sheet 'Head, shoulders, knees and toes' on page 11 and ask them to point to the different body parts as they sing the song. Supply scissors and glue so that they can cut out the labels at the bottom of the page and stick them in the appropriate place on the picture. Support them if necessary.
● Create a 'Body parts' display (see page 75) by drawing round a child, cutting out the resulting outline and fastening it to a low wallboard. Invite the children to attach clothing and create facial features from collage materials. Label the display with the body parts mentioned in the song and choose someone to point to them while singing.

Differentiation
Ask younger children to stand in a circle to sing the song so that they can learn the names of body parts, and their sequence in the song, by watching and listening to others. Encourage more able children to make up new versions of the song, for example, 'Neck, elbows, heels and wrists'.

ON THE CD-ROM
● Photocopiable sheet 'Head, shoulders, knees and toes'

Head, shoulders, knees and toes

| head | shoulder | knee | toe |

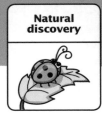

themes for early years

Mirror activities

What you need
Small safety mirrors; small and large pieces of mirror card (available from educational suppliers); adhesive tape; the photocopiable sheet 'Mirror images' on page 13.

Preparation
Make concave and convex mirrors by bending large pieces of mirror card. Use adhesive tape to fix them in position, or stick them on to the inside and outside of half a cardboard tube as shown.

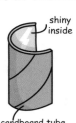

shiny inside

adhesive tape

shiny outside

cardboard tube

shiny inside

shiny outside

What to do
Ask the children to work with a partner and give each pair a small safety mirror. Suggest that they take turns to look into the mirror and describe their reflection to their friend. Supply each child with a safety mirror and a copy of the photocopiable sheet and ask them to see what happens when the mirror is held along the dotted lines of each picture. Suggest that the children take turns to look into concave and convex mirrors made from mirror cards. What happens to their reflection with each one?

Discussion
How much of their bodies can the children see in a mirror? Does this change if they stand near or far away from the mirror? Which body parts move if they wave or wink? Compare the properties of the mirror card with those of the safety mirrors. How well do they reflect? Name other items in which the children have seen their reflections, such as spoons and kettles. Discuss how mirrors are used for various purposes, for example, on cars or at the dentist.

Follow-up activities
- Sing the song 'I'm alive shanty' on page 79 and then sing it while looking into mirrors to observe the body parts mentioned.
- Set up a hairdressing table with safety mirrors, brushes, hair ornaments and small hats. Have fun creating different reflections.

Differentiation
Let younger or less able children work individually, and talk them through their actions. Give more able children two pieces of mirror card and challenge them to arrange them together in different positions.

Mirror images

themes for early years

STEPPING STONE
Differentiate marks and movements on paper.

EARLY LEARNING GOAL
Explore colour, texture, shape, form and space in two or three dimensions. (CD)

ASSESSMENT
Note the children's ability to observe and follow an adult demonstration of colour blending techniques. Provide more support to individuals if necessary.

Self-portraits

What you need

Safety mirrors; two framed portrait photographs; grey sugar paper; charcoal; chalks or pastels; scissors; glue sticks; fixative spray.

What to do

Listen to the rhyme, 'That's my face', on the CD-ROM before supplying each child with a safety mirror to observe their reflections. Encourage them to concentrate on their faces, naming and describing the various parts.

Ask the children to use chalk and charcoal to draw large pictures of their faces on grey sugar paper. Show them how to blend colours by smudging with their fingers and create new colours by overlapping.

Show the children the portrait photographs and discuss how they are framed. Supply narrow strips of grey sugar paper and help the children to measure and cut them to the right length to form frames around their portraits. Stick the frames to the portraits. Once the children have left the room, spray the portraits with fixative (following the manufacturer's instructions).

Display the finished portraits and discuss them with the children.

Discussion

Focus the children's attention on their facial features, for example, by talking about the colour of their eyes, the shape of their noses and the length and texture of their hair. Talk about distinctive features such as freckles, hair ornaments or earrings. What sort of expressions will they draw on their faces? Compare a photograph with a drawing. Describe how each one is made and find similarities and differences between them.

Follow-up activity
● Show the children two different self-portraits, painted by famous artists in the past, and explain that photographs were not available in those days. Compare and contrast the two portraits. You could start by identifing the various body parts. Then discuss the appearance of each portrait, for example, sex, age, physical attributes, clothing and hairstyle. Talk about the feelings conveyed by the portraits. What else can we tell about the people portrayed?

Differentiation

Create a selection of ready-made cardboard frames for younger or less able children to choose from. Encourage more able children to create textured frames using collage materials such as buttons, sequins and seeds.

ON THE CD-ROM
● Poem 'That's my face'

ICT

themes for early years

Welcome albums

What you need
Digital camera; computer; printer; photograph albums; large envelopes; sticky tape.

What to do
Talk to the children about the activities they have enjoyed during a session. Which body parts did they use? Did they play by themselves or with other children? Suggest making some photograph albums depicting busy children in different play areas to help them to consider how they use their bodies.

Make a list of play areas in the room and concentrate on one area for a full session. Demonstrate how to take photographs using a digital camera and ask an adult to spend time in the area encouraging children to take photographs of themselves at play.

Print out the photographs and store them in a large envelope before moving to another play area the next session.

Work on one envelope of photographs with a small group of children. Decide upon a suitable print for the album cover and tape it into place before arranging the other photographs on the album pages.

Go through the album together, writing down the children's caption ideas related to body movements for each photograph, for example, 'Kate and Naseem used their strong arms and hands to lift the heavy jugs'. Type and print the captions and stick them under the appropriate photographs.

Work with different groups of children until all of the albums are completed. Display the finished albums in appropriate play areas and encourage the children to look at them with friends and families.

Discussion
Talk about the difference between tiny finger movements and whole body movements. Discuss which photograph the children liked most, for example, a picture of two children blowing bubbles together or climbing up the ladder of a slide.

Follow-up activities
- Make an album entitled 'Using our bodies' to stimulate conversation between parents and children.
- Make a digital camera readily available and encourage children to take photographs of favourite three-dimensional work to put into their record files.
- Say or listen to the rhyme 'That's my face' on page 90.

Differentiation
Look at the albums with shy children to encourage them to try something new. Encourage more able children print their photographs and type their own captions.

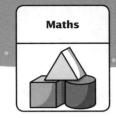

Maths

themes for early years

Matching bodies

What you need
Pictures of people from different nationalities cut from magazines; card; adhesive plastic film; scissors; adhesive; a globe.

Preparation
Mount the pictures on separate pieces of card and cover with adhesive plastic film. Cut each picture into two horizontally.

What to do
Mix up the picture pieces and ask children to match the top halves to the appropriate bottom halves. Discuss similarities and differences between the resulting people.

Explain that the people in the pictures live in different countries and use a globe to locate these countries. Discuss how the children would travel from their homes to visit each person.

Discussion
Encourage the children to identify the common physical characteristics of the people, such as hands and eyes, and then look for individual differences, for example, in age, gender, physical appearance, expression and clothing. Is it possible to determine from background details whether they live in a hot or a cold country? The children's concept of the wider world will vary considerably. Look at a globe with them and identify basic physical features such as sea and land.

Follow-up activities
- Make a copy of the photocopiable sheet 'Tops and bottoms' on page 17 for each child, mount it on card and cut out the individual pieces. Invite the children to match 'tops' and 'bottoms' to create pictures of four children and then make comparisons between them.
- Invite children to complete the CD-ROM activity 'Tops and bottoms' by matching the lower and upper halves of the babies, children and adults on the computer screen.

Differentiation
Begin with pictures of two contrasting people, and gradually add more pictures as younger or less able children become increasingly confident. Invite more able children to choose one aspect of physical appearance for comparison, such as eye or hair colour, and ask them to record similarities and differences between the people they have created from the cut-out pictures.

ON THE CD-ROM
- On-screen activity 'Tops and bottoms'
- Photocopiable sheet 'Tops and bottoms'

Tops and bottoms

ICT

themes for early years

Face puzzles

STEPPING STONE
Gain an awareness of the cultures and beliefs of others.

EARLY LEARNING GOAL
Begin to know about their own cultures and beliefs and those of other people. (KUW)

ASSESSMENT
Observe the way that individual children match the pictures, and note their comments about similarities and differences, so that the activity can be extended or simplified if necessary to ensure progression of skill and knowledge.

What you need
Simple puzzle pictures of faces; digital camera; card; glue sticks; adhesive plastic film; scissors.

What to do
Ask the children to work in pairs, each pair completing a puzzle together. When they have finished, ask the children to compare the pictures on the puzzles. Suggest that they make their own face puzzles.

Invite the children to take turns to use a digital camera to take a close up photograph of the face of their partner. Print off the photographs and mount them on card.

Cover the children's photographs with adhesive plastic film and suggest that they cut each image into a few large pieces.

Invite the children to piece their own puzzle back together and then swap puzzles with other members of the group.

Discussion
Ask the children to describe the faces of their partners using the puzzles. Encourage them to talk about eye colour, length of hair, skin colour and so on. Sensitively discuss additional features such as glasses, hairbands or hearing aids. Talk about how well the puzzles work. Which is the easiest one to do? Which is most difficult and why? How could this difficult puzzle be made easier next time?

Follow-up activities
● Give the children a copy of the photocopiable sheet 'Jigsaw faces' on page 19 each. Can they name the parts that are missing? Ask them to draw lines to match the missing puzzle pieces at the bottom of the page to the empty spaces.
● Print copies of the photograph of a child's face on the CD-ROM and invite the children to create a jigsaw following the 'What to do' section above.

Differentiation
Take the photographs for younger or less able children, and help them to cut along two or three bold lines to simplify the puzzle-making process. Supply more able children with a copy of the photocopiable sheet and invite them to cut out the missing facial features at the bottom of the page and stick them into the correct empty spaces.

ON THE CD-ROM
● Photograph of a child's face
● Photocopiable sheet 'Jigsaw faces'

Jigsaw faces

STEPPING STONE
Begin to differentiate between past and present.

EARLY LEARNING GOAL
Find out about past and present events in their own lives, and in those of their families and other people they know. (KUW)

ASSESSMENT
Listen to the children's comments and note how well they are able to differentiate between past and present.

Baby match

What you need
Two photographs of each child, one as a baby and one at present; small plastic wallets; small pieces of card; felt-tipped pens.

Preparation
Put each photograph into a small plastic wallet. Write the child's name on a small piece of card and slide it behind the matching photograph with the name facing inward. Make a set of separate name cards.

What to do
Turn the child photographs upside down in their plastic wallets and invite each child to turn one over, look at it carefully and then describe it to the others. Ask the others to guess who is in the photograph before revealing the name underneath. Repeat this with the baby photographs.

Ask the children to find their own names from the set of name cards and put them next to their photographs.

Discussion
Encourage the children to look at the photographs and discuss how they have changed. What is different about their physical appearance? Are there any differences in clothing? Is it easier to match some baby to child photographs because of obvious similarities, such as the same red hair or expression. Compare the baby photographs. Is it possible to tell which is the youngest or oldest baby? Now compare the present day photographs. Have the children all grown to the same size?

Follow-up activities
● Read the poem 'Once I was a baby' on page 91 to stimulate the children's memories of the past.
● Suggest that the children think of words to describe their photographs. Create a display with the photographs, names and captions, positioned near to the role-play area to stimulate play based on past and present experiences.

Differentiation
Simplify the activity initially by just using photographs of younger or less able children as they are now rather than as babies. Extend the activity for more able children by asking each child to match the photographs and name card for someone else in the group.

ON THE CD-ROM
● Poem 'Once I was a baby'

What do I wear?

This chapter focuses on naming and describing a wide range of clothing, and discusses why and when these clothes would normally be worn.

themes for early years

Dressing up

Role play

What you need
A selection of dressing-up clothes to appeal to both sexes; large boxes; labels; felt-tipped pens; large safe mirror; digital camera; writing paper; pencils; glue sticks; card; small plastic box; scissors.

Preparation
Invite the children to sort the dressing-up clothes into boxes according to the type of clothing, for example, hats, belts and shirts. Attach a simple word and picture label to each box. Cut the card into rectangles so they stand upright in the small plastic box, allowing enough space for a photograph and a brief written description. Label the box appropriately, for example, 'Abracadabra, look how I have changed!'

What to do
Read or listen to the rhyme 'Dressing up' on page 90 to stimulate discussion about dressing-up clothes that the children like wearing. Invite the children to change their appearance using the dressing-up clothes. When they are satisfied with their outfits, take a digital photograph of each child saying 'Abracadabra', adopting a pose and expression to match their clothing. Print the photographs, mount them onto the prepared cards and ask individual children to dictate or write a brief description of what they are wearing and the type of character they have become. Store the 'Abracadabra' cards in the plastic box.

Discussion
Encourage children to describe the colours and textures of their clothes, and any decoration. Ask them to identify common materials such as wool and leather. Invite the children to assess their changing appearance in the mirror. Discuss the reasons for their choices.

Follow-up activities
● Use the 'Abracadabra' cards for storytelling and sorting activities.
● Create role-play dressing up boxes or 'Abracadabra' cards.

Differentiation
Help younger or less able children to fasten difficult clothing. Invite more able children to decide what sort of character is emerging as they dress up. What physical mannerisms would this character have?

ON THE CD-ROM
● Poem 'Dressing up'

themes for early years

STEPPING STONE
Examine objects and living things to find out more about them.

EARLY LEARNING GOAL
Find out about, and identify, some features of living things, objects and events they observe. (KUW)

ASSESSMENT
Observe the ability of individual children to identify objects by touch alone so that you can meet the varying needs of the group and ensure steady progression.

What's in the bag?

What you need
A drawstring bag; five or six items of clothing such as a hat, belt, shoe, jumper, swimsuit and pair of shorts.

Preparation
Place the items of clothing inside the bag without the children seeing them.

What to do
Explain that the bag contains items of clothing. Invite the children to take turns to put one hand into the bag, choose an article to describe, identify it by touch alone and then pull it out to see if they have guessed correctly.

Change the items once the children are familiar with them.

Discussion
Encourage each child to describe the item they are touching in detail, and use questions to extend their descriptive abilities. Does it stretch or bend? What kind of material is it made out of? Can you feel any fastenings? Is it rough or smooth? Discuss when and why each garment would be worn. Is it suitable for hot or cold weather? Would it be worn every day, or on a special occasion?

Follow-up activities
● Make a copy of the photocopiable sheet 'Find the pairs' on page 23 for each child. Invite the children to cut out the pictures at the bottom of the sheet and sort them into three piles, 'socks', 'gloves' and 'footwear'. Then ask them to match three of the pictures to the objects inside the bag to create matching pairs.
● Demonstrate how to operate the CD-ROM activity 'What's in the parcel'. Encourage the children to discuss the parcel shapes and guess what might be inside them before dragging them down to cover the appropriate toy at the bottom of the screen.

Differentiation
Ensure that younger or less able children achieve success by reducing the number of items in the bag and choosing garments of contrasting size, shape and texture. Increase the level of difficulty for more able children by including two similar items, for example, a rain hat and a bobble hat, and see if the children can distinguish between the two.

ON THE CD-ROM
● On-screen activity 'What's in the parcel?'
● Photocopiable sheet 'Find the pairs'

Find the pairs

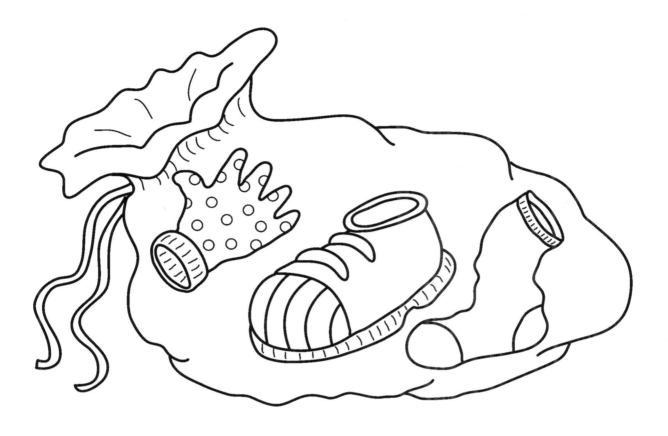

Sound

themes for early years

Clapping clothes

What you need
Five or six articles of clothing such as a skirt, belt, trainers, sari, petticoat and cardigan.

What to do
Say the rhyme 'Clapping clothes' on page 92 and listen to the CD-ROM version to stimulate the children's awareness of sound patterns in words.

Ask the children to sit in a circle with the articles of clothing in the middle. Select a child to choose and name an item of clothing. Demonstrate how to clap the name of the item with one clap per syllable and ask the children to join in. Repeat this for each item of clothing.

Once the children are familiar with this, clap the rhythm for the name of each garment as it is held up and ask the children to say the name.

Finally, invite them to say the name and clap the rhythm without you.

Discussion
As the name of each garment is clapped, ask the children to count the number of claps. Which clothes have most or fewest claps? Which ones have the same number? How many items of clothing can the children suggest for two claps? Can they suggest something for four claps?

Follow-up activities
- Clap simple rhythms involving one, two or three claps, and ask the children to suggest an item of clothing to fit that rhythm.
- When the children are dressed in their outdoor clothing suggest that they clap the rhythms of the garments they are wearing, such as coats, jackets, mittens and hats.

Differentiation
If younger or less able children find clapping a difficult co-ordination task, suggest they slap their knees instead. Invite more able children to play a circle clapping game. Ask them to take turns to name and clap the rhythm for any item of clothing while the rest of the group copy these actions. Suggest that each child chooses a different item of clothing.

ON THE CD-ROM
- Poem 'Clapping clothes'

themes for early years

Shoe mimes

What you need
A collection of contrasting footwear, such as Wellington boots, football boots, high-heeled shoes, ballet shoes, tap shoe; tambourine and beater; large safe outdoor space.

What to do
Take the children outdoors and warm-up by asking them to pretend to shake their shoes off, both on the spot and while on the move.

Display the collection of shoes in a row and ask the children to name each type. Explain that they are going to pretend to put each pair on and move about in them.

Invite the children to take turns to choose a pair of shoes for everyone to mime to. Use the tambourine to accompany their movements and to signal the start and finish. Try to vary the sound created to match the chosen shoe, for example, banging loudly, brushing gently, shaking softly or tapping the edge with the sharp end of a beater.

Discussion
Encourage the children to explore their own movement ideas before broadening their range by introducing more structured suggestions. For example:

Wellington boots – stamping in mud, jumping in puddles, dragging through water, kicking piles of dead leaves.

Football boots – running or jogging in various directions at different speeds, kicking, dribbling, jumping to head a ball.

High heels – walking on tiptoes, walking daintily around mud or puddles, falling over.

Ballet shoes – leaping and gliding, twisting and turning, moving high and low with pointed toes.

Tap shoes – experimenting to make as many different sounds as possible, both loud and soft, with different parts of their feet.

Follow-up activities
- Put the pairs of shoes into a box and challenge the children to find the matching pairs as quickly as possible.
- Create a 'Shoe prints' display, see page 76.
- Sing the song 'Shoe choose tune' on page 80, adding appropriate actions, or play the CD-ROM version for the children to dance to.

Differentiation
Present younger or less able children with just two contrasting pairs of shoes, such as Wellington boots and ballet shoes. Invite more able children to work in pairs, one playing the tambourine and one miming.

STEPPING STONE
Move spontaneously within available space.

EARLY LEARNING GOAL
Move with confidence, imagination and in safety. (PD)

ASSESSMENT
Notice how well individual children use the space around them. Do they move confidently or hesitantly? Do they copy others or use their own imaginations?

ON THE CD-ROM
- Song 'Shoe choose tune'

ICT

themes for early years

STEPPING STONE
Order two or three items by length.

EARLY LEARNING GOAL
Use language such as 'greater', 'smaller', heavier' or 'lighter' to compare quantities. (MD)

ASSESSMENT
Observe whether the children managed to complete the activity easily within a specific time. If difficulties arose, could these be overcome in future?

Socks on the washing line

What you need
A large piece of card; felt-tipped pens; eight socks of different lengths.

Preparation
On the card draw a straight washing line between two large posts, large enough to 'hang' the socks on.

What to do
Invite the children to handle the socks freely before focusing their attention on the length of each one. Show them the picture of the washing line, explain that the socks have blown off it and challenge them to return them in order, from the shortest to the longest.

After completing the practical activity, set up the 'Hanging out the washing' activity on the CD-ROM for pairs of children to try. Demonstrate how to drag the socks onto the washing line in size order.

Discussion
Encourage the children to describe the colour, texture and decoration of each sock. Would a child or an adult wear the sock? Does it have a particular function, such as a football sock or a Christmas stocking? Ensure that the children realise that a true comparison of size can only be made if the socks have a common starting level. Demonstrate this with two socks on the washing line picture, emphasising the need for the top of each sock to touch the straight line.

Follow-up activities
● Hand out copies of the photocopiable sheet 'Hang them out' on page 27 and invite the children to cut the socks out and work independently to arrange them in size order along the washing line.
● Read the rhyme 'Patterns in socks' on page 94, or listen to the CD-ROM version, before encouraging children to consider similarities and differences in their own socks.
● Invite the children to paint giant socks with interesting patterns, and challenge more mature children to devise repeat patterns. Cut the socks out and mount them in order of length on a picture of a washing line. Make the socks easily detachable, so they can be mixed up and reordered correctly.

ON THE CD-ROM
● On-screen activity 'On the washing line'
● Poem 'Patterns in socks'
● Photocopiable sheet 'Hang them out'

Differentiation
Use just three or four socks of obviously different sizes for younger or less able children. Challenge more able children by increasing the number of socks or reducing the time allowed to complete the task.

Hang them out

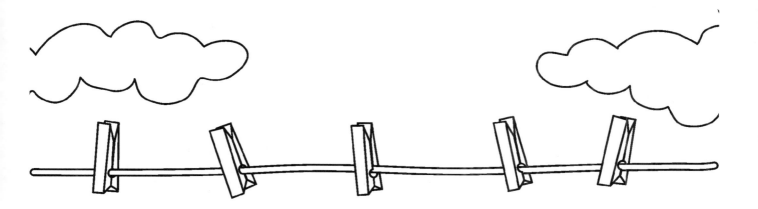

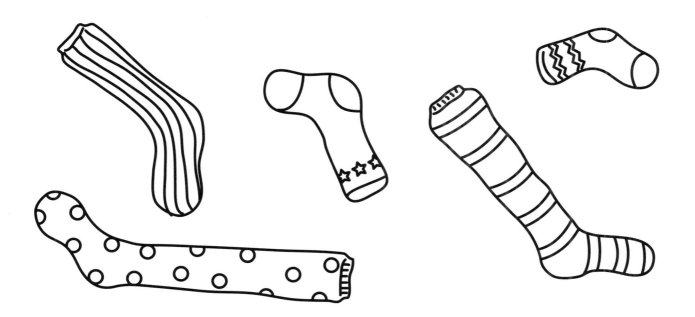

Hat game

STEPPING STONE
Show an interest in the world in which they live.

EARLY LEARNING GOAL
Observe, find out about and identify features in the place they live and the natural world. (KUW)

ASSESSMENT
Establish children's awareness of the roles of the people who would wear the hats used in the activity by listening to their comments and observing their actions.

What you need
Six hats associated with jobs, for example, a builder, firefighter, police officer, crossing patrol person, cook and postal worker; individual pictures of people wearing the uniforms associated with the hats (remember to find a balance of male and female representatives); six small boxes, large enough for each hat to sit on; six pieces of paper in different colours; sticky tape.

Preparation
Cover each box in different coloured paper and tape a picture of a worker to one side.

What to do
Display the boxes on a table with the pictures facing the front so that the children can see them clearly.

Identify the occupations of the people and talk about their clothing, especially their hats.

Pass around the hats and invite the children to match them to the pictures by placing the correct one on top of each box.

Discussion
Talk about the function of the clothing worn by the people. Why does a fire-fighter need leggings? How does a fluorescent tabard help a crossing patrol person? Invite the children to describe the size, colour, shape and weight of each hat. Discuss how the design and materials used help the person perform their job. Why does a cook need a hat? Why is a policeman's helmet hard?

Follow-up activities
● Provide each child with a copy of the photocopiable sheet 'Match the hats' on page 29. Talk about the people and hats depicted, and ask the children to draw a line to match the correct hat to each person.
● Sing the song 'That hat!' on page 80, or listen to the CD-ROM version, and supply the children with different hats to use as props as they join in.

Differentiation
Encourage younger or less able children to play with the hats and talk to them about who might wear the hat. Support them in appropriate role-play actions. Challenge more able children by concealing the head of each person on the pictures with small circles of coloured paper before finding the appropriate hat for them.

ON THE CD-ROM
● Song 'That hat!'
● Photocopiable sheet 'Match the hats'

Match the hats

● Match the hats to the people.

firefighter

builder

police
officer

crossing
patrol
person

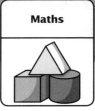

Maths

themes for early years

Baby clothes

What you need
A selection of baby clothes; clothing suitable for a child; small suitcase; baby doll; two labels; felt-tipped pens; two set rings.

Preparation
Put the items of clothing into the small suitcase. Make two labels, 'Clothes for a baby' and 'Clothes for us'.

What to do
Pass around a baby doll and explain that some of the clothes in the suitcase are suitable for the doll and some for a child.

Place the two set rings on the floor with a label in each. Sit the doll near the appropriate label to help the children distinguish which ring is which. Challenge them to sort the items of clothing in the suitcase into the correct rings.

Discussion
After sorting the clothes, talk about each item in turn. Name the article and decide which part of the body it fits. Discuss the size, shape, colour, texture and decoration. Talk about the differences between the clothes for a baby and those for a child. As well as discussing obvious differences in size, can the children identify changes in development? For example, compare the nappy with the pants.

Follow-up activities
- Show the children the photograph of the baby and child on the CD-ROM and discuss visible differences. Invite them to bring in photographs of themselves showing what they wore as a baby and what they wear now.
- Provide each child with a piece of paper with two large rings drawn on it labelled 'When I was a baby, I wore . . .' and 'Now I am four, I wear . . .' Ask the children to draw clothes, or stick pictures from clothing catalogues, inside the correct rings.

Differentiation
Simplify the activity for younger or less able children by asking them to differentiate between two similar items of doll's clothes in contrasting sizes, such as a 'little' dress and a 'big' dress. Challenge more able children to sort clothing for dolls of three different sizes, using appropriate language such as, 'small', 'smaller' and 'smallest' or 'big', 'bigger' and 'biggest'.

ON THE CD-ROM
- Photograph of a baby and child

Birthday badge

STEPPING STONE
Persist for extended periods of time at an activity of their choosing.

EARLY LEARNING GOAL
Maintain attention, concentrate, and sit quietly when appropriate. (PSED)

ASSESSMENT
Ensure that necessary materials are at hand to enable children to become fully motivated and then note the length of time individual children are able to concentrate.

What you need
A collection of badges showing different ages; different coloured card; pencils; scissors; colouring media, such as wax crayons, coloured pencils and felt-tipped pens; Velcro; adhesive tape.

What to do
Show the children the badges and discuss their size, shape, colour, decoration and construction. Sing the birthday song 'This day is a special day' on page 86.

Identify the numbers on the badges and establish the age of each child in the group. Suggest that the children make their own badges and invite them to discuss possible designs.

Let each child choose a piece of coloured card, draw and cut out the overall badge shape and draw on the relevant number for their age. Provide a choice of media for the children to decorate their badges. Help each child to stick a piece of Velcro to the back of the finished badge.

Discussion
As the children handle and discuss the badge collection, encourage them to state their age and the date of their birthday. Look for similarities in the badges, and suggest that the children sort them into sets, for example, with the same shape, colour, or number. As the children suggest potential badge designs, encourage them to name the materials they want to use. What size and shape will they choose? How will they decorate them? Demonstrate how Velcro can be used to 'stick' the badges onto some articles of clothing and help the children to fix them to an appropriate garment.

Follow-up activities
- Invite the children to invent different ways of fixing a card badge, avoiding any damage to their own clothes by using old clothes from the dressing-up box if necessary. Offer them string, thick wool, ribbons, paper-clips, treasury tags, hairclips, pipe-cleaners and small bulldog clips.
- Make badges to support other occasions, such as cultural events and festivals.

Differentiation
Cut out badge shapes and provide stick on numerals so that younger or less able children can concentrate on the task of decorating them. Invite more able children to describe how they made their badges and assess the advantages and disadvantages of the design.

ON THE CD-ROM
- Song 'This day is a special day'

Who shares my home?

The people with whom young children live are an important focus in their daily lives, and can provide the theme of many exciting activities.

Family portraits

What you need

Photographs of the children's families; white paper; black pens.

What to do

Ask the children to name and describe the people in their family photograph and help them to establish the relationships between them. Sensitively approach any emotional family circumstances, for example, involving divorce, bereavement or re-marriage.

On white paper with black pens ask the children to draw a large picture of their family group. Refer them to the photographs for details of physical appearance and clothing. They may include additional family members if they wish to. Label and display the finished pictures.

Discussion

Encourage children to make comparisons between the appearances of the people in their photographs. Who is the tallest, or shortest? What clothes are they wearing? Questions such as these will help children to include more details in their drawings. Experiment with the different marks the children can make with the pens. Can they create long curved lines to represent hair? When the pictures are displayed, ask each child to talk about their family portrait to the rest of the group.

Follow-up activities
- Show the children the family photographs on the CD-ROM and sensitively discuss similarities and differences between them.
- Invite the children to compose a group poem about a relative and scribe their individual ideas. Choose the relative wisely, so that all children are able to contribute.

Differentiation

Supply younger or less able children with large crayons or short thick paintbrushes to draw or paint their portraits. Suggest that more able children use the pens to create dark areas on their family portraits by colouring in or shading, and to use thin brushes to add a small amount of water to selected areas to blur the lines.

STEPPING STONE
Have a sense of belonging.

EARLY LEARNING GOAL
Have a developing respect for their own cultures and beliefs and those of other people. (PSED)

ASSESSMENT
Are the children able to differentiate between family members and talk confidently about the roles they play in their lives?

ON THE CD-ROM
- Photograph of family of six
- Photography of family of three

themes for early years

STEPPING STONE
Observe and use positional language.

EARLY LEARNING GOAL
Use everyday words to describe position. (MD)

ASSESSMENT
Do the children understand the symbols 1st, 2nd, 3rd and 4th? Are they able to follow them in the correct sequence?

Family treasure hunt

What you need
Four pieces of card; felt-tipped pens; four small world characters.

Preparation
Hide the four characters (to represent a family) in various places, indoors or outdoors, without the children seeing. Draw a simple picture on each piece of card to give a clue about where each one is hidden. Label the cards '1st', '2nd', '3rd', '4th', and write the name of the appropriate family member on each (see illustration).

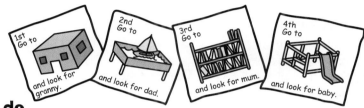

What to do
Explain to the children that the toy family has got lost and needs to be found. Show them the cards in turn and explain that the numbers represent the order in which they must look for the toys. Ask them to identify the picture symbol for the place where the toy is hidden, and help them to read the name of the family member. Mix up the cards and ask the children to sequence them correctly. Can they find the toys in the correct order? Support them if necessary. When the children return with the toys, ask them to sequence the cards again and place the correct toy on top.

Discussion
Make sure the children understand the ordinal aspect of numbers by asking them to form a line and call out their respective positions. Ask them to identify the place pictured on each card and then point to it as it is recognised. Invite the children to describe the place where they are searching, using as much positional language as possible and to describe the exact position of the toy when it is found.

Follow-up activities
● Repeat the activity in other locations with new sets of cards to retain the children's motivation.
● Set up an obstacle course with large apparatus, such as benches, planks, tunnels and barrels, and plan out a route with the children using positional vocabulary.

Differentiation
Reduce the number of cards and toys to simplify the activity for less able or younger children. Invite more able children to design their own treasure hunt, inventing new picture symbols to represent places in their environment.

themes for early years

Pets

What you need

Three-sided screen; small tables; soft toys to represent pets, such as hamsters, mice, rabbits and guinea pigs; plastic model snakes, spiders and lizards; cardboard boxes; plastic fish tanks; pet cages and baskets; shredded paper; blankets; books and posters about pets; pet accessories such as toys and empty food packets; till; toy money.

What to do

Ask the children about their experiences of pets. Have they ever visited a pet shop? What did they buy? Suggest setting up a role-play pet shop using the resources suggested above.

House the toy pets in boxes, cages and tanks and label each one. Use shredded paper and blankets as bedding.

Display the books, pet toys and accessories on the tables and hang the posters on the screens.

Discussion

Look at the CD-ROM photograph of the child and dog, and the film clip of the child with a guinea pig, to encourage the children to talk about their own experiences of pets. Encourage the children to play freely in their shop and visit as a customer to buy a pet to stimulate discussion about different types of pet. Ask questions about pet care, housing, food and toys.

Follow-up activities
● Provide the children with copies of the photocopiable sheet 'The pet shop' on page 35 and invite them to cut around the individual pictures. Put the pictures of the dog, cat and goldfish in a row and then choose which items on the remaining pictures would be suitable for each pet and arrange them alongside.
● Sing the song 'Pets' on page 82, or listen to it on the CD-ROM, and then make up new verses naming the children and their pets.

Differentiation

Invite the parents of younger or less able children to supply a photograph of their child's pet as a starting point for discussion. Encourage more able children to create labels and price tags for the items for sale in their shop.

STEPPING STONE
Begin to use talk to pretend imaginary situations.

EARLY LEARNING GOAL
Use language to imagine and recreate roles and experiences. (CLL)

ASSESSMENT
Listen to the language used by individual children as they play in the shop. Are they able to develop imaginary scenarios and draw upon their own experiences?

ON THE CD-ROM
● Film clip of a child with guinea pig
● Photograph of a child with his dog
● Song 'Pets'
● Photocopiable sheet 'The pet shop'

The pet shop

themes for early years

Crossing safely

What you need
A carpeted area; a roll of wallpaper; a black felt-tipped pen; a large and small doll and teddy bear.

Preparation
Unroll the wallpaper upside down on the carpet. Place the large teddy bear and doll at one end and the small teddy bear and doll at the other. Use the black pen to draw a large simple maze connecting the toys, similar to that on the photocopiable sheet. Make sure the pathways are large enough for the children to 'walk' the small teddy bear and doll along and that there are several alternative pathways.

What to do
Gather the children around the maze and make up a story in which the small teddy bear and doll feel very sad because they have become separated from their parents while out walking.

Make sure that the children realise which toy matches which parent, then ask them to look carefully at the maze to find a pathway from the child to the adult. Suggest that a volunteer tries to 'walk' the small teddy bear to the parent, and repeat this with the small doll.

Discussion
Encourage the children to give each teddy bear and doll a name. Have the children ever been lost? Can they describe how the toys feel? Discuss what children should do if they get lost, and the problems of 'stranger danger'.

Follow-up activities
● Use the photocopiable sheet 'Safely home' on page 37 to consolidate this activity. Ask the children to use a pencil to draw in the route for each toy, making sure their pencil lines do not bump into the edges of the pathway.
● Ask children to work in pairs, each drawing their own maze and offering it to their partner to find the way through.

Differentiation
Make a straightforward path using carpet tiles and invite younger or less able children to find their way from one end to the other. Challenge more able children to find alternative routes from toy to matching adult. Which is the longest or shortest route?

Safely home

● Draw a route home for the small doll and teddy.

themes for early years

Dressing a doll family

What you need
Three dolls of contrasting sizes; clothing for each doll.

What to do
Pass around the undressed dolls before inviting the children to give them names and suggest the family relationships between them, for example, a mother and two daughters or a mother, son and grandmother.

Make up a story in which the dolls' clothes have become muddled up, and ask the children to work in pairs to dress one of the dolls in the correct clothing. Repeat the activity by swapping the dolls between pairs of children.

Discussion
Talk with the children about each item of clothing. What is it called? Which part of the body does it go on to? How does it fasten? What material is it made of? Is it suitable for hot or cold weather? Encourage the children to predict which clothes will fit their dolls before they try them on. Use comparative vocabulary such as 'too big', 'smaller than', 'not big enough' and 'largest'. Discuss the order in which the clothes should be put on. Is it better to put trousers on before or after underwear? Is one particular item of clothing more difficult to put on than the rest? Ask the children to compare dressing dolls with dressing themselves at home or before physical activities. What do they find most difficult and why?

Follow-up activities
- Give the children a copy of the photocopiable sheet 'Match the clothes' on page 39. Make sure that they recognise each item of clothing and ask them to draw a line to match the items to the correct part of the body for each doll. Remind them to take size into account when allocating the clothing.
- Invite a parent to bring in a baby for the children to watch as the baby is undressed, bathed and dressed again.

Differentiation
Ensure that the dolls' clothes have easy fastenings such as Velcro or elastic to simplify the activity for younger or less able children. Extend the activity with the photocopiable sheet by asking more able children to draw another item of clothing in three appropriate sizes for the dolls.

STEPPING STONE
Engage in activities requiring hand-eye coordination.

EARLY LEARNING GOAL
Handle tools, objects, construction and malleable materials safely and with increasing control. (PD)

ASSESSMENT
Note how much support individuals need with this activity and plan further similar activities to strengthen fine motor skills if necessary.

ON THE CD-ROM
- Photocopiable sheet 'Match the clothes'

Match the clothes

● Can you match the clothes to the people?

Grandad   Mum   Baby

ICT

Dangers at home

What you need
A set of 'safe' objects that could be found in the home, for example, wooden bricks, books, teddy, plastic cup; a set of 'unsafe' objects, for example, sharp scissors, a knife, an electric plug, a hand-held electric mixer; two set rings; two labels, one marked 'safe' in green, one marked 'unsafe' in red.

What to do
Talk to the children about how some objects at home can be dangerous and should be handled by adults only. Can they think of any examples? Put the two set rings on the floor, adding the 'safe' label to one and the 'unsafe' label to the other. Explain what each label means.

Show the children the objects and ask them to take turns to point to one of them and instruct an adult which set to put it into.

When all of the objects have been classified discuss where they might be found in the home and what they might be used for.

Discussion
Talk about each object as it is classified into a set. What is it? Is it safe or unsafe? Why? Stress the need for children to follow simple safety rules involving unsafe objects, for example, not touching plugs. Devise an appropriate set of rules for the home, for example, within the kitchen, 'We never touch the kettle', or 'We never play with matches'.

Follow-up activities
- Invite the children to explore the photocopiable sheet 'Keeping safe' on page 41, point out the kitchen hazards, draw a ring round each one and give reasons for highlighting it.
- Read the rhyme 'Keeping safe' on page 95, or listen to it on the CD-ROM, as a starting point for discussion about appropriate behaviour and the consequences of actions.

Differentiation
Encourage younger or less able children to paint a picture of one of the dangerous objects before helping them to write a suitable caption. Invite more able children to create a poster about safe behaviour within the home.

ON THE CD-ROM
- Poem 'Keeping safe'
- Photocopiable sheet 'Keeping safe'

Keeping safe

Mark-making

themes for early years

Birthdays

What you need

Blue sugar paper; a black felt-tipped pen; white drawing paper; pencils; crayons; dark blue backing paper; glue stick; coloured wool; a stapler.

What to do

Ask the children how they celebrate their birthdays and write down a list of their comments on a sheet of blue sugar paper, for example, 'get birthday cards', 'sing "Happy Birthday"', 'have parties'. Watch the film clip together and talk about what the children can see at the celebration. Talk about how different members of the children's families celebrate their birthdays. Do siblings, parents and grandparents celebrate in the same way? Use the list as a focus for discussion.

Give each child a square piece of white paper folded into four. In the top left quarter, ask the children to draw and colour a picture of their birthday celebration. Under this, ask them to dictate one or two sentences describing what is happening. In the other spaces, invite the children to draw a picture of another family member's birthday celebration, with a brief description.

Cover a display board with dark blue paper and staple the list and the children's pictures to it. Invite children to colour balloon shapes and stick them to blue sugar paper strips to form a border. Tape wool strings to each balloon and staple around the display (see illustration).

STEPPING STONE
Have an awareness of, and show interest and enjoyment in, cultural and religious differences.

EARLY LEARNING GOAL
Understand that people have different needs, views cultures and beliefs, that need to be treated with respect. (PSED)

ASSESSMENT
Do the children show by their comments that they realise that there are differences in birthday celebrations across ages and cultures?

Discussion

Encourage the children to identify similarities and differences between age groups when celebrating birthdays. Help them realise that there are many ways of celebrating, but each one represents an important landmark in life.

Follow-up activities

● Make a display to show the month in which each child was born.
● Sing 'This day is a special day' on page 86, or listen to it on the CD-ROM, when a child celebrates a birthday.

ON THE CD-ROM
● Film clip of a birthday party
● Song 'This day is a special day'

Differentiation

Ask younger or less able children paint a large picture of their birthday celebration and add a caption for them. Invite more able children to make birthday cards for their friends so that each child can choose one on his/her birthday.

themes for early years

Visitors

STEPPING STONE
Use talk, actions and objects to recall and relive past experiences.

EARLY LEARNING GOAL
Use talk to organise, sequence and clarify thinking, ideas, feelings and events. (CLL)

ASSESSMENT
Listen to way the children use language during discussions. Are they able to make links between their experiences and the topic for discussion or do they rely on the objects provided to stimulate their memories?

What you need
A selection of items that visitors to the children's houses might wear or carry, for example, a child's bobble hat, a flat cap, a parcel, a handbag, a bucket and a pair of strong leather gloves.

What to do
Show the children a selection of items similar to those suggested above and explain that they were all left behind by visitors to your house. Can they guess who the visitors might be? Go through them one by one and explain who left them.

Ask the children about visitors who come to their homes and make a graph with the children's names along the bottom and the visitors down the side. Are there any visitors who regularly call at all of their houses, for example, the window cleaner? Who calls at some, but not all, of the houses?

Discussion
Talk about regular social visitors such as friends, family members and neighbours. How far do they have to travel? Do they sometimes sleep over? Who is the children's favourite visitor? Ask the children to think of visitors who care for them, such as doctors and childminders.

Follow-up activities
- Make a set of cards, each one depicting a visitor in distinctive clothing, and invite the children to take turns to pick a card and then pretend to be that visitor knocking on the door and making up an appropriate mime. Invite the others to ask questions to try and decide who the visitor might be.
- Sing the song 'Visitors' on page 83, or listen to it on the CD-ROM, and then invite the children to join in with appropriate actions.

Differentiation
Invite regular family visitors, such as grandparents, to visit the setting with younger or less able children to support them in discussions during this activity. Suggest that more able children create a book about their visitors. Invite them to bring in photographs and draw pictures, and scribe captions for them.

ON THE CD-ROM
- Song 'Visitors'

The activities in this chapter use the children's increasing physical and intellectual achievements skills as a basis for developing work in all areas of the curriculum.

Helping

ICT

What you need
A digital camera; printer; card; PVA glue; laminator; set of name cards.

Preparation
Ask two children to help you to take a photograph of each play area, print the photographs, mount them on card and laminate them.

What to do
Explain that you would like the children to be 'Happy helpers' at tidy up time. Ask the two 'photographers' to show the others the cards they have created and explain how they were made. Identify the play area depicted on each one. Arrange the cards upside down on a table and put a box of name cards alongside.

Choose a child to pick a card and then choose a friend or two to help to tidy the area depicted on it. Return the card to the table with the photograph upwards and ask the chosen children to find their name cards and put them alongside. Continue until all of the cards and names have been allocated and then ask the 'Happy helpers' to begin tidying.

Discussion
Talk about the tasks involved in being 'Happy helpers', such as picking up equipment and sweeping sand. After the children have tidied, ask them to talk about the things they did in their designated areas.

Follow-up activities
- The photocopiable sheet 'Happy helpers' on page 45, is a board game mount it on card and laminate it. Explain that the game is about 'Happy helpers' tidying up. Children to choose their own counter and read out instructions related to moving forward extra squares when helpful tasks are undertaken.
- Read the rhyme 'Happy helpers' on page 92, or listen to it on the CD-ROM, and discuss things that children can do to help others.

Differentiation
Spend time with younger or less able children demonstrating how to tidy up each play area. Ask more able children to partner younger children to demonstrate how to handle, tidy and care for equipment.

---

themes for early years

STEPPING STONE
Know how to operate simple equipment.

EARLY LEARNING GOAL
Find out about and identify the uses of everyday technology and use information and communication technology and programmable toys to support their learning. (KUW)

ASSESSMENT
Listen to the children's comments about making the photograph cards in order to assess individual awareness of the use of technology to support activities.

ON THE CD-ROM
- Photocopiable sheet 'Happy helpers'
- Poem 'Happy helpers'

Happy helpers

You pour out
the drinks.
Move 2

You wipe
the table.
Move 1

You wash
the cups.
Move 1

You help
to tidy
the books.
Move 3

You put
away the
train set.
Move 1

You mop
up some
water.
Move 1

You tidy
the home
area.
Move 2

You pick up
some beads.
Move 3

Start
to tidy up
here.

Outdoor environment

themes for early years

Experimenting with beanbags

What you need
Beanbags; large open space; record sheet (see illustration); pencils.

What to do
Ask each child to choose a beanbag and then find five different ways of making it travel a short distance.

Encourage the children to discover their own methods of moving the beanbag, rather than copying each other. Their suggestions might include balancing it on part of their own body, such as the head, neck, shoulder, elbow, back of hand, knee or foot, while moving, throwing it, kicking it, sliding it along the ground or pushing it along the ground with different parts of their body.

Give each child a pencil and a record sheet (as shown in the illustration) and suggest they record each method after they have devised it. Depending on the age of the children, an adult could act as scribe or the children could draw pictures or write brief descriptions.

With a bean bag, I can...

Discussion
If the children are unfamiliar with bean bags, it is useful to ask them to describe the bags in detail, for example, talking about shape, size, colour, texture, smell and weight before beginning the activity. Allow a short time for each child to show and describe the ideas they have recorded on the sheet to the other members of the group. Highlight similarities and differences in their methods.

Follow-up activities
● Suggest that the children choose one of their methods for moving the beanbag and paint or draw a picture of themselves using it. Combine the pictures to make a class frieze.
● Ask the children to count the beanbags and write the number in the box on the photocopiable sheet 'Beanbags' on page 47.
● Repeat the activity, but with a different piece of small apparatus such as a ball or hoop.

Differentiation
Simplify the activity for younger or less able children by asking them to take turns to balance a beanbag somewhere on their body and then position the beanbag in the same place on a life-size outline drawing of a child. Suggest that more able children find additional ways to move the beanbag and continue their recording on the reverse side of the sheet.

ON THE CD-ROM
● Photocopiable sheet 'Beanbags'

Myself

Beanbags

Mark-making

themes for early years

What I can do

What you need
White paper; felt-tipped pens; coloured paper; pencils; crayons.

What to do
Read the poem 'I can' on page 88 aloud, or listen to it on the CD-ROM, and discuss it with the children, identifying the achievements mentioned. Repeat it several times, encouraging the children to join in and add actions.

Suggest that the children compose a group 'I can' poems and ask them to think of things that they can do. List their ideas on a large sheet of white paper.

Hang a second sheet of paper beside the first and write 'I can...' as a title. Invite each child to choose an idea from the list, or suggest a new one, and make up a short sentence for the poem. There is no need for words to rhyme.

Read the resulting poem several times, modifying vocabulary and helping children to remove unnecessary words. Write out the finished poem, with each line on a separate piece of paper, and mount it on coloured paper. Ask each child to draw a small picture to illustrate their line, and use these to decorate the poem.

Recite the poem and encourage the children to devise actions to accompany it.

Discussion
When composing their poem, encourage the children to think of original ideas rather than repeat those in the poem they have heard. Vary the time spent improving the poem according to the concentration span of the group.

Follow-up activities
● Form individual 'caterpillar' achievement records based on activities undertaken. Ask each child to suggest a different achievement to be written on a coloured gummed circle and stuck to a caterpillar's head.
● Make an 'Action words' display, see page 77.

Differentiation
Encourage younger or less able children to demonstrate their physical achievements, such as jumping or waving, and describe these actions in words. Invite more able children to identify the rhyming words in the poem on page 88.

ON THE CD-ROM
● Poem 'I can'

Mark-making

My hands

What you need
Three everyday objects such as a book, hat and plastic beaker; white paper; pencils; crayons; coloured card; finger paints; PVA glue.

What to do
Place the objects on a table and invite the children to take turns to try to pick something up without using their hands. Discuss how difficult life would be without hands.

Suggest that the children make individual zigzag books about hands. Supply each child with four small pieces of white paper and ask them to draw a different picture of themselves using their hands on each one. Invite them to dictate or write a sentence describing their actions on four separate small pieces of paper.

Fold strips of coloured card into zigzags and ask each child to make handprints on one strip. When the prints are dry, stick the pictures and text on to the pages to form a book. Write the title and name of the author on small pieces of white paper and stick these to the front cover.

Encourage each child to read their book to the group, and then display them for others to read.

Discussion
Inspire ideas by talking about ways in which we use our hands in everyday life. Name parts of the hand and discuss how they are used in various actions. Ask the children about the importance of their hands in performing the printing activity. Could they put on aprons or mix paints without using their hands?

Follow-up activities
- Sing favourite finger and hand rhymes, and encourage the children to identify the various movements their hands and fingers are making.
- Sing the song 'With my hands' on page 79 and the rhyme 'Tommy Thumb' on page 87, and listen to them on the CD-ROM to inspire further discussion.

Differentiation
Ask younger or less able children to draw one picture with a caption and use them to form a group book. Invite more able children to make detailed comparisons between the handprints with a magnifying glass. How do they differ?

ON THE CD-ROM
- Song 'With my hands'
- Poem 'Tommy Thumb'

themes for early years

Mark-making challenge

STEPPING STONE
Further explore an experience using a range of senses.

EARLY LEARNING GOAL
Respond in a variety of ways to what they see, hear, smell, touch and feel. (CD)

ASSESSMENT
Observe whether individuals use the sense of touch, hearing and smell as well as sight when describing their clay, and encourage them to do so if necessary.

What you need
Clay; rolling pins; collection of tools, such as a clay modelling tool, toothbrush, comb, twig, fir cone and screw; small pieces of card; felt-tipped pens.

What to do
Invite the children to choose a piece of clay and flatten it with a rolling pin.

Show them the tools, naming each one, and ask them to choose one to press into their clay to make different marks. Continue to experiment with more pieces of clay.

Invite the children to choose their favourite piece of clay to display on a table, marking their initials on the underside. Arrange the tools in spaces between them, not necessarily next to corresponding clay pieces.

Make a card label for each piece of clay, with the name of the child on one side and a picture of the tool used on the reverse. Place the correct label, with the name facing upwards, next to each piece.

Invite the children to guess which tool made the marks on each piece of clay and then check by turning over the card.

Discussion
Invite the children to describe the appearance, smell and feel of the clay, and the sounds made when rolling and marking it. Encourage children to experiment with all parts of their chosen tool and describe the marks they produce. Compare the finished pieces of clay. How many different marks were produced with each tool? Which tool made the most? Are any the same? Which piece of clay do the children prefer and why?

Follow-up activities
- Repeat the activity using another media, such as paint, and a different range of tools.
- Encourage the children to make comparisons between how Plasticine, play dough and clay look, smell and feel.
- Sing 'With my hands' on page 79 to promote discussion about how they used their hands.

Differentiation
Supply younger or less able children with pliable play dough to work with rather than stiff clay. Invite more able children to look for suitable everyday objects to use as tools, emphasising that they need to check with an adult before using them.

ON THE CD-ROM
- Song 'With my hands'

Construction
and malleable
materials

themes for early years

Working together

What you need
Collection of plastic construction equipment, including a large
baseboard.

What to do
Invite the children to sit in a circle on the carpet, and explain that they
are going to work together to build a model.

Place the construction equipment in the middle of the circle, then
give one child the baseboard. Ask the child to choose a construction
piece, fix it to the base board and say what it is, for example, a house, a
box or a bridge.

Pass the baseboard on to the next child to add another piece and
name the new structure. Each child can put their own interpretation on
the developing model, or the group may decide to work towards the
same idea, such as a castle or bus.

Continue around the circle, at least until all of the children have had
a turn.

Discussion
Talk with the children about the colour, size and shape of the
construction pieces they choose. Encourage children to use positional
language by asking them about where they decide to place their pieces,
for example, 'on top', 'beside', 'in between'. If appropriate, count the
number of pieces that have been used. Talk about other activities the
children can do collectively. Which do they enjoy most and why?

Follow-up activities
● Make some prompt cards to be used with the construction toys,
for example, 'Can you build a house with ten bricks?' Invite the
children to choose a card and attempt the given task.
● Use a recycled box as a base and take turns to glue something to
it to create a group abstract model.

Differentiation
Choose larger construction pieces that are easy to grip and manipulate
if children are younger or less able. Invite more able children to draw
plans of their chosen construction and decide together how they will set
about building it.

themes for early years

STEPPING STONE
Remember and talk about significant things that have happened to them.

EARLY LEARNING GOAL
Find out about past and present events in their lives, and in those of their families and other people they know. (KUW)

ASSESSMENT
Listen to children talking about their activities and note whether they are aware of differences between past and present.

Our day

What you need
Four large sheets of white paper; felt-tipped pens; card; two tables.

Preparation
Label one sheet of paper for each time period, 'morning', 'afternoon', 'evening', 'night' and divide each sheet of paper into six rectangles.

What to do
Read 'Daily routines' on page 95. Discuss activities the children enjoyed yesterday, reminding them of the date. What can they remember doing during each time period? Suggest that they make a picture display depicting these activities.

Show them the four labelled sheets and suggest that they all dictate one activity for each time period and then illustrate each sentence using the felt-tipped pens.

Mix up the finished sheets and ask individual children to sequence them correctly.

Arrange the sequenced sheets across two tables and write 'Our day' on a stand-up card with the appropriate day and date alongside. Encourage the children to explore the pictures freely and practise sequencing them.

Discussion
Ask each child to think of a different activity. Is the activity something they do daily, or is it specific to yesterday? As they suggest activities, reinforce the order of the time periods by talking about which one comes first, second and so on.

Follow-up activities
● Make copies of the photocopiable sheet 'My day' on page 53, mount them on card and cut out the sections. Invite the children to sequence the pictures to follow a day in the life of the boy or girl.
● Read the poem 'Bedtime in summer' on page 89, or listen to it on the CD-ROM, to stimulate discussion about memories of seasonal differences.

Differentiation
Invite younger or less able children to draw a picture of the activity that they have enjoyed most during a session and display the pictures as a frieze. Help more able children to make a weekly diary, recording one activity each day. At the end of each daily session choose one child to draw a picture of an important activity for that day and write a brief sentence underneath to describe the activity.

ON THE CD-ROM
● Poem 'Bedtime in summer'
● Photocopiable sheet 'My day'
● Poem 'Daily routines'

My day

themes for early years

Body sounds

What you need

Tape recorder; blank cassette.

What to do

Explain to the children that they are going to make some body sounds. These could include clapping hands, slapping knees, stamping feet, tapping toes or heels, rubbing hands together, or a range of voice sounds.

Make a sound yourself and ask the children to join in one at a time as you move around the circle. Repeat this with one or two more body sounds and then ask individuals to suggest other sounds. Introduce the idea of loud and soft sounds and ask the children to identify them.

Extend this activity by making a sequence of body sounds. Demonstrate one or two yourself for the children to copy, and then ask individuals to make up their own for the group to copy. Encourage them to combine loud and soft sounds.

Invite each child to make up a short sequence of body sounds to be recorded on a cassette.

Discussion

When the children are making sounds as a group, encourage them to maintain an even rhythm. Talk about the different methods they are using to make sounds. Which sound is loudest or softest? Which sound do they like least or best? Encourage the children to describe the sound sequence they are making. Which part of the body is being used? How many sounds are being made? Discuss the recorded sequences, identifying individual body sounds.

Follow-up activities

● Challenge the children to invent body sounds to accompany a favourite story.
● Read the poem 'Animal sounds we can make' on page 89, or listen to it on the CD-ROM, before asking the children to invent their own animal sounds.

Differentiation

Help younger or less able children to operate recording equipment. Encourage more able children to work together to record their sound sequences without adult support.

STEPPING STONE

Explore and learn how sounds can be changed.

EARLY LEARNING GOAL

Recognise and explore how sounds can be changed, sing simple songs from memory, recognise repeated sounds and sound patterns and match movements to music. (CD)

ASSESSMENT

Observe whether individual children try out body sounds of their own or rely on others for ideas.

ON THE CD-ROM
● Poem 'Animal sounds we can make'

How do I feel?

This chapter looks at emotions such as happiness, sadness, anger and fear and shows how to help young children cope and find appropriate ways of expressing their feelings.

Worry tree

What you need
Small branch; coloured paper; hole punch; thin ribbon; plant pot; clay.

Preparation
Fill the pot with clay and push the branch into it to resemble a small tree. Cut coloured paper into small rectangles and punch a hole in the corner of each one.

What to do
Introduce the word 'worry' and encourage children to express their own concerns by referring to your own worries. Explain that sharing a worry can help and invite individuals to share a worry with the rest of the group. Emphasise that this is voluntary, and sensitively respond to confidences so that no child feels uncomfortable.

Suggest turning the tree you have made into a 'worry tree' where children can hang worries to be discussed later. Write a worry you used as an example earlier on a piece of paper. Thread ribbon through the hole and tie it around the branch. Invite children to come to you throughout the session if they would like to dictate a worry to hang on the tree. Read the worries at the end of the session, with individuals if more appropriate, and discuss how they might be overcome.

Discussion
Support children verbally as they expand upon worries. Encourage children to approach staff members individually if this is more comfortable for them.

> ### Follow-up activities
> ● Read or listen to the poem 'My worries' on page 91, to emphasise the importance of sharing worries with an adult.
> ● Make a book called 'Our worries', containing drawings and captions.

Differentiation
Invite younger or less able children to hang their names on the tree instead. Take them off in turn and talk about what they liked or disliked in that session. Explain to more able children how being a good listener can help when friends are worried, and practise these skills with them.

themes for early years

STEPPING STONE
Express needs and feelings in appropriate ways.

EARLY LEARNING GOAL
Respond to significant experiences, showing a range of feelings when appropriate. (PSED)

ASSESSMENT
Listen to children's comments to ascertain their confidence when expressing anxieties.

ON THE CD-ROM
● Poem 'My worries'

Mark-making

Happy and sad news

STEPPING STONE
Begin to break the flow of speech into words.

EARLY LEARNING GOAL
Use their phonic knowledge to write simple regular words and make phonetically plausible attempts at more complex words. (CLL)

ASSESSMENT
Observe whether children break their sentences down into individual words and use their knowledge of phonics to support them as they write.

What you need
Two sample letters; pencils; crayons; writing paper; envelopes; stamps.

Preparation
Write and post two sample letters to yourself, one containing happy news, such as the birth of a child, and the other containing sad news, such as a relative moving house.

What to do
Explain that you received two letters in the post and that one made you sad and one made you happy. Read the letters aloud and ask the children to identify the emotion provoked by each.

Invite the children to describe occasions when they, or members of their families, have received happy or sad letters.

Discuss the conventions of letter writing, using your letters and envelopes as examples. Ask the children to point to the address, stamp and date on the envelopes and the address, date, opening phrase and closing phrase on the letters.

Suggest that the children write a happy or sad letter to someone at home. When the letters are finished, place them in envelopes, put on a stamp and take them to the post-box. Encourage parents to write back to their children to provide an added dimension to the project.

Discussion
As you help the children to write words in their letters, or scribe for them, draw attention to the letter sounds involved. Suggest that the children read their finished letter to a friend and identify whether it contains happy or sad news. Encourage the children to bring in any replies to their letters to share with the group.

Follow-up activities
● Read the poem 'Happy news, sad news' on page 94, or listen to it on the CD-ROM, to stimulate discussion about contrasting events in the children's lives.
● Talk about the person who delivers the post and the work of the Post Office.

Differentiation
Have an adult scribe for younger or less able children, supporting them with vocabulary suggestions. Encourage more able children to attempt to write simple regular words using their phonic knowledge.

ON THE CD-ROM
● Poem 'Happy news, sad news'

themes for early years

The happiest day of my life

What you need
Photograph of a happy time in your life; white drawing paper; pencils; crayons; coloured paper; PVA glue; stapler.

What to do
Show the children your photograph and tell them it portrays a happy day in your life. Ask them to describe what they can see in the photograph. Can they deduce what the situation or event is?

Ask each child to think of the happiest day in their life and describe it to the group, for example, a birthday, a wedding, the birth of a sibling, a religious or cultural celebration, a party, an outing or a holiday.

Suggest that each child draws and writes about their happiest day. Mount the finished work on coloured paper and staple the sheets together to form a book entitled 'The happiest day of my life'.

Discussion
Ask the children why this particular time was the happiest day in their life. Who shared this special day? Help the children develop their sense of time by trying to relate the 'happiest day' to other events. Was it in winter or summer, this year, last year or a long time ago? How old were they? Ask whether something they could bring in to show the group as a record of their day, for example, a photograph, greetings card or ticket to a special place.

Follow-up activities
● Look at the photograph of a family celebrating the Jewish festival of Passover on the CD-ROM. What are the people doing? How are they dressed? Do the children have experience of a similar event in their own lives?
● Watch the CD-ROM film clip about a birthday party to stimulate memories of the children's own birthday celebrations.
● Listen to and sing along to the songs 'This day is a special day' and 'Jump for joy' on the CD-ROM or on page 86 and 84, respectively.

Differentiation
Invite parents of younger or less able children to send in a photograph of a recent happy event in their child's life so that they have something tangible to stimulate their memories. Encourage more able children to compile a list of simple, everyday things that make them happy, such as a hug or sharing a game with a friend.

STEPPING STONE
Display high levels of involvement in activities.

EARLY LEARNING GOAL
Continue to be interested, excited and motivated to learn. (PSED)

ASSESSMENT
Listen to the children to ascertain their ability to recall past events in detail.

ON THE CD-ROM
● Film clip of a birthday party
● Photograph of a family celebrating Passover
● Song 'This day is a special day'
● Song 'Jump for joy'

themes for early years

Things that scare me

STEPPING STONE
Have a positive self-image and show that they are comfortable with themselves.

EARLY LEARNING GOAL
Understand that they can expect others to treat their needs, views, cultures and beliefs with respect. (PSED)

ASSESSMENT
Note any fears expressed by the children so that you can support them in future situations.

What you need
Copy of the photocopiable sheet 'Little Miss Muffet' on page 59 for each child; card; PVA glue; crayons; scissors.

Preparation
Mount a copy of the photocopiable sheet on card for each child and cut out the two slots as indicated. Prepare some strips of card, the same length as the sheet and just wide enough for the children to slide them through the slots and move them up and down easily.

What to do
Provide each child with a prepared copy of the 'Little Miss Muffet' sheet and invite them to colour Little Miss Muffet and the spider.

Ask the children to cut out their spiders and glue them to the centre of one of the prepared strips of card.

Show them how to slide each end of the strip through the slots at the top and bottom of the page so that the spider sits in the middle. Demonstrate how to move the spider to frighten Little Miss Muffet by sliding the strip up and down from the back of the sheet. Say the rhyme 'Little Miss Muffet' together, asking the children to make their spiders move up and down at the appropriate moment.

Discussion
Talk about Little Miss Muffet's fear of spiders. Are the children frightened of anything? Positively encourage them to express their fears by explaining that being frightened is nothing to be ashamed of.

Follow-up activities
● Invite the children to try the CD-ROM activity, 'Little Miss Muffet', moving the spider up and down the screen with the mouse to see Little Miss Muffet lift her arms in fright when the spider touches her.
● Play with toy spiders and stick them to webs made from grey wool to help allay children's fears.

ON THE CD-ROM
● On-screen activity 'Little Miss Muffet'
● Photocopiable sheet 'Little Miss Muffet'

Differentiation
Prepare the sheets beforehand for younger or less able children so that they can use them as props for the rhyme. Encourage more able children to tackle all aspects of the activity, including cutting and sticking.

Little Miss Muffet

Art and craft

themes for early years

Friendship

What you need

Card; wool in contrasting colours; clear contact adhesive; hole punch; crayons or felt-tipped pens.

Preparation

Cut the card into strips long enough to wrap around a child's wrist with room to tie the ends together with wool. Cut coloured wool into strands of around 10cms.

What to do

Look at the photograph on the CD-ROM showing some good friends hugging each other and encourage discussion about the importance of friendship. Suggest that children make bracelets as presents for special friends.

Demonstrate to the children how to colour a strip of card on both sides with a design of their choosing and cover it in contact adhesive for protection.

Punch a hole at either end of the strip and show the children how to thread woollen strands in contrasting colours through each hole to tie the bracelets in place.

Discussion

When the children have chosen someone to make a bracelet for, encourage them to give reasons for their choice. Why is this friend so special? Ask the children about their choice of design and colours and invite them to explain to others how they made their bracelet.

Follow-up activities

- Make copies of the photocopiable sheet 'Friendship bracelets' on page 61 and ask the children to colour the patterns to stimulate awareness of mathematical symmetry. Transform the strips into bracelets using the above method.
- Read the rhyme 'Best of friends' on page 93, or listen to it on the CD-ROM, to emphasise that friends can have differences.
- During the Hindu festival, Raksha Bandhan, explain the tradition of sisters honouring their brothers by making wristbands for them and invite the children to make bands for their siblings using the above method.

Differentiation

Help younger or less able children to make friendship hats rather than bracelets by colouring strips of card to tape around their heads. Invite more able children to make a book about friendship, starting by making a list of desirable attributes.

STEPPING STONE

Notice what adults do, imitating what is observed and then doing it spontaneously when the adult is not there.

EARLY LEARNING GOAL

Use their imagination in art and design, music, dance, imaginative and role play and stories. (CD)

ASSESSMENT

Note whether children are able to follow a simple practical demonstration or need extra support with techniques such as cutting and punching holes.

ON THE CD-ROM
- Photograph of a group of friends
- Photocopiable sheet 'Friendship bracelets'
- Poem 'Best of friends'

Friendship bracelets

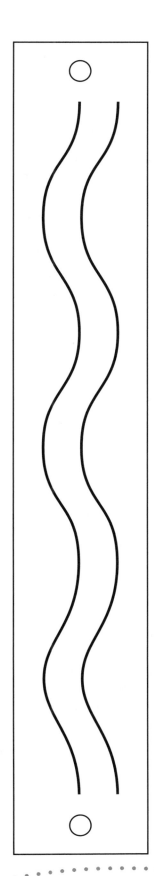

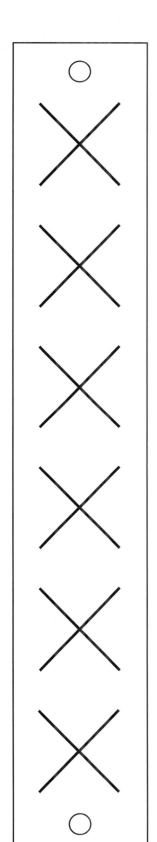

Sound

Happy and sad music

themes for early years

STEPPING STONE
Try to capture experiences and responses with music, dance, paint and other materials or words.

EARLY LEARNING GOAL
Express and communicate their ideas, thoughts and feelings by using a widening range of materials, suitable tools, imaginative and role play, movement, designing and making, and a variety of songs and musical instruments. (CD)

ASSESSMENT
Listen to children's comments and observe their expressive movements to identify whether these change appropriately with the moods of the music.

What you need
Examples of short pieces of music evoking happy and sad moods; tape recorder.

What to do
Play each piece of music to the children to identify whether it makes them feel happy or sad. What is it about the music that makes them feel this way?

At the end of the discussion, play all the pieces of music through without interruption.

Discussion
Talk about how each piece of music makes the children feel. Encourage spontaneous responses such as clapping or tapping hands and body movements. Ask the children to consider how each mood is created. Which instruments are being used? Do they hear one sound at a time or lots of sounds together? Identify whether sounds are fast or slow, loud or quiet, high or low, longer or shorter. Are there periods of silence?

Follow-up activities
- Offer the children a wide selection of percussion instruments, such as woodblocks, tambourines, claves, drums, Indian bells, triangles and maracas, to accompany the different pieces of music. Which instruments create a happy sound? Which ones provide a suitable accompaniment for sad music?
- Print off the photographs of a happy and sad face from the CD-ROM, mount them on card and put them on the floor side by side. Invite the children to sit around them and point to the appropriate photograph to match the music they hear.

Differentiation
Play younger or less able children two contrasting pieces, one to provoke excitement and one to create a calm atmosphere, and invite them to move freely to each one. Ask more able children to work in pairs to compose their own short piece of music using percussion instruments and tuned instruments, such as a xylophone or glockenspiel, to reflect an emotion of their choice. Record their compositions, replay them to the children and evaluate the results.

ON THE CD-ROM
- Photograph of a smiling girl
- Photograph of a sad boy

themes for early years

STEPPING STONE
Have a positive approach to new experiences.

EARLY LEARNING GOAL
Be confident to try new activities, initiate ideas and speak in a familiar group. (PSED)

ASSESSMENT
Note whether children join this new activity with confidence and manage to express their ideas clearly to others.

Good moods

What you need
Large drawstring bag; children's choice of objects from around the room; percussion instrument.

What to do
Sit in the story corner and explain that you are in a 'good mood' today because, for example, your sister has had a baby. Show the children a real object related to this news, such as an item of baby clothing.

Contrast this by telling children about an event from yesterday that put you in a 'bad mood', for example, spilling a box of breakfast cereal on the floor. Again show something tangible, such as the empty cereal box.

Ask children about their own good and bad moods and the reasons for them.

Hold up the drawstring bag and explain that it is a 'Good mood' bag and you need to put things into it.

Explain that you will play an instrument towards the end of the session and demonstrate how this sounds. On hearing the instrument, ask the children to find one object each to put into the 'Good mood bag' to remind them of something that made them feel particularly happy during that session.

Explore the bag contents together and ask each child to give reasons for their choice of object.

Discussion
Ask children to think of words to describe a good mood, for example, 'happy', 'bubbly', 'fizzy', and contrast this with words describing a bad mood, such as 'sad', 'hurting', 'cross', 'angry'.

Discuss how children can help one another to feel happy when they are sad, for example, with a smile or by inviting them to join their play.

Follow-up activities
● Make 'Good mood' music recordings to liven everyone up at the start or end of a session.
● Think of other moods that children experience, such as 'anger', 'surprise' or 'disappointment', and discuss their cause.

Differentiation
Encourage younger or less able children to recognise how choices influence moods by asking them to indicate favourite activities. Invite more able children to make a 'Good mood' display using the objects in the bag with card captions alongside explaining who chose them and why.

themes for early years

STEPPING STONE
Observe the effects of activity on their bodies.

EARLY LEARNING GOAL
Recognise the changes that happen to their bodies when they are active. (PD)

ASSESSMENT
Listen to the children's comments and note whether they can explain the body changes they feel after exercise.

Jump for joy

What you need
A portable CD player; a carpet tile or square for each child.

Preparation
Spread the carpet squares around the available space, leaving room for the children to move easily in and out of them.

What to do
Invite the children to sit on a small carpet square each while they listen to the song 'Jump for joy' on page 84 and the CD-ROM. Talk about the meaning of the words 'Jump for joy' and discuss each verse in turn. Would the events mentioned make the children want to jump for joy? Can they think of other happy times when they would feel like this?

Play the song again, asking the children to jump freely up and down with feet together on the carpet squares.

At the end of the song ask the children to stand still and talk about any changes they notice in their bodies. Are their hearts beating faster? Do they feel out of breath?

Repeat the song, this time asking the children to jump all around the available space. Is it harder to jump around or to jump on the spot?

Discussion
Listen to the first verse and discuss how weather can alter how we feel. Do the children enjoy running in the wind? How do they move on a cold wet day? Listen to the verses about special celebrations. Which celebrations do the children enjoy most? Can they say why? Why does visiting friends make us jump for joy?

Follow-up activities
● Make up movements based on feelings, for example, hopping with happiness, stamping with anger or rolling with laughter.
● Use the carpet squares to play 'musical statues', asking the children to dance to music on the CD-ROM and find a square to stand on, as still as a statue, when the music stops.

Differentiation
Support younger or less able children by holding their hands as they jump. Explain to more able children how the heart and lungs work during exercise.

ON THE CD-ROM
● Song 'Jump for joy'

This chapter looks at how diet, exercise, hygiene, road safety and daily routines all form important parts of young children's lives.

Wash your hands

Water

themes for early years

What you need
A water tray; protective clothing; paper towels; four bars of soap of the same colour; three bars of soap in different colours.

What to do
Gather the children around the water tray and discuss the importance of washing regularly. Invite them to choose a friend to share the activity. Give each pair a bar of soap in the same colour, and ask them to describe the appearance and smell and how it feels.

Ask them to put their bar of soap in the water tray, leave it for a few minutes and describe what happens to it. Use a dry bar of soap for comparison.

Invite the children to use the bars of soap to make a bubbly lather on their hands and ask them to describe the colour of the bubbles.

Allow them to repeat the activity with the different-coloured soaps, predicting and then testing to see what colour the bubbles are.

Discussion
Talk about when the children should wash their hands, for example, after going to the toilet, before eating or after a messy activity. When comparing the wet and dry soaps, ask the children to describe any changes in colour, smell or texture. What happens to the water around the soap?

Follow-up activities
- Read the rhyme 'Hand washing' on page 95, or listen to it on the CD-ROM, to raise the children's awareness of when to wash their hands.
- Design a sign to display in your setting to remind everyone to wash their hands.

Differentiation
Help younger or less able children to find hand washing enjoyable by leaving items associated with hygiene near the water tray for free play activities. Encourage more able children to support their younger friends by reminding them when they need to wash their hands.

ON THE CD-ROM
- Poem 'Hand washing'

Food

themes for early years

STEPPING STONE
Use some number names and number language spontaneously.

EARLY LEARNING GOAL
Use developing mathematical ideas and methods to solve practical problems. (MD)

ASSESSMENT
Note whether children use appropriate mathematical language when making links between the number of fruits and the number of beads on the laces.

Eat more fruit

What you need

A selection of fruits; apron; knife; small plates; beads; laces; card; hole punch; felt-tipped pens.

Preparation

Cut out some small pieces of card and draw and colour a picture of a fruit from the selection on each one. Punch a hole in each card and thread a lace through it, securing the end with a knot so that the card will not fall off.

What to do

Ask the children to wash their hands and put on an apron before exploring the fruits freely. How many can they name?

Cut the fruits in half and discuss differences between the inside and outside. Invite the children to taste bite size pieces of each fruit. Ask each child to decide which fruit tastes best, then ask them to choose a bead and thread it onto a prepared lace displaying the picture of their favourite fruit.

Compare the numbers of beads on the laces to discover the most or least popular fruit.

Discussion

Encourage the children to describe the colour, shape, texture and smell of each fruit. Sort the fruits according to colour, size or shape. Find words to describe the taste of each fruit. Do the children know why eating fruit is 'good for you'? How often do they eat fruit? Ask questions about the bead tally. Do more children prefer bananas than prefer apples? How many more choose grapes than choose melon? Do any fruits have the same tally?

Follow-up activities
- Invite the children to try the 'Healthy meal' activity on the CD-ROM asking them to choose from options on the screen, and click on those that will make a healthy meal.
- Try a range of fruit including bananas, apples and kiwis. Reinforce one-to-one correspondence using the photocopiable sheet 'Draw and count' on page 67.
- Identify and discuss the fruits on the photograph on the CD-ROM.

Differentiation

Help younger or less able children to name the fruits. Encourage more able children to arrange the fruits in order from the least to the most popular.

ON THE CD-ROM
- On-screen activity 'Healthy meal'
- Photograph of a fruit stall
- Photocopiable sheet 'Draw and count'

Draw and count

● Draw a banana for each child.

● Draw an apple for each child.

● Draw a kiwi fruit for each child.

Art and craft

Skeletons

What you need

A picture or model of a skeleton; black paper; white paper, drinking straws, matchsticks, pipe-cleaners, wool and string; scissors; PVA adhesive; glue sticks.

What to do

Show the children the picture or model of a skeleton and help them to identify the various bones.

Talk about the way in which bones serve as a framework for our bodies. Emphasise the need to care for bones through a healthy diet and exercise. Invite the children to make skeleton collages on black paper. Suggest that they choose suitable materials from those provided, and cut or tear them to make appropriate shapes to stick on to the paper. Refer them back to the picture or model for details.

Display the collage pictures alongside the model or picture of a skeleton.

Discussion

As the parts of the skeleton are identified, suggest that the children feel for the bones in their own bodies. Can they feel their ribs, skulls or collarbones? Count the number of bones in an arm or leg on the model. Why do we need ribs or a skull? What would happen if our bones didn't grow properly or got broken? As the children make their collages, ask them to justify their choice of materials. Which materials could be used for ribs or finger-bones? Which are flexible or rigid? How can each material be changed, for example, by cutting, tearing or bending, to suit the image of a skeleton? Discuss the type of pose their skeleton will adopt. Will it be waving, jumping or dancing? Allow time to talk about the finished collages. Which ones do the children prefer and why?

Follow-up activities

- Invite the children to dance like skeletons to the 'Fossils' movement from *Carnival of the Animals* by Saint-Saens.
- Read 'Tommy Thumb' on page 87 or sing 'Jump for joy' on page 84 or listen to them on the CD-ROM. Then use these to introduce a discussion about what bones you are using.

Differentiation

Cut materials into small manageable pieces for younger or less able children to handle. Supply more able children with recycled materials, such as tubes and boxes, and suggest that they make a three-dimensional skeleton on a large sheet of card.

STEPPING STONE
Investigate construction materials.

EARLY LEARNING GOAL
Build and construct with a wide range of objects, selecting appropriate resources, and adapting their work where necessary. (KUW)

ASSESSMENT
Note whether children choose appropriate materials independently and if they are aware of appropriate joining techniques.

ON THE CD-ROM
- Rhyme 'Tommy Thumb'
- Song 'Jump for joy'

Outdoor environment

Hoop game

STEPPING STONE
Judge body space in relation to spaces available when fitting into confined spaces or negotiating holes and boundaries.

EARLY LEARNING GOAL
Show an awareness of space, of themselves and of others. (PD)

ASSESSMENT
Observe whether children are able to negotiate the increasingly reduced space available without causing problems for themselves and others.

What you need
A plastic hoop for each child; tambourine.

What to do
Explain to the children that regular exercise keeps every part of the body in working order.

Warm up by asking the children to shake every part of their bodies while you shake the tambourine. Provide the children with a hoop each to put on the floor and stand inside. Explain that they are going to exercise different parts of their bodies while moving around the hoops without touching them.

Shake the tambourine as a signal to start and tell the children which body parts to move, for example, 'two feet and one arm'. When the tambourine is silent ask them to find a hoop to stand in.

Repeat the activity, with different body movements, removing a hoop each time and allowing more than one child to stand in a hoop. Continue until only two or three hoops are left.

At the end of the activity, discuss the effect of exercise on the children's bodies.

Discussion
Naming the parts of the body to be exercised, instead of specifying movements such as hopping or clapping, will enable children's movement responses to be more open-ended. Praise those who think of unusual ways of moving. At the end of the session, ask the children which body parts have not been exercised. How has exercise changed their bodies? Are they hot and sweaty? Are their hearts beating faster?

Follow-up activities
- Collect pictures of people involved in different sports and exercise activities, such as football, swimming, tennis, aerobics and ice skating. Discuss each activity and describe which parts of the body would be used most.
- Read the rhyme 'Quiet as mice' on page 87 and invent appropriate actions.

Differentiation
Leave the same number of hoops out for the whole activity if children are younger or less able. Invite more able children to take the part of the adult, shaking the tambourine and calling out body parts to be moved.

ON THE CD-ROM
- Poem 'Quiet as mice'

Food

themes for early years

Milkshake

What you need

Ingredients: a 410g tin of unsweetened apricot halves in fruit juice; 4 tablespoons natural yoghurt; 600ml milk; cornflakes for decoration. Equipment: tin opener; tablespoon; clear plastic jug; mixing bowl; hand whisk; apron, knife, small plate, fork, plastic beaker and straw for each child; blender or food processor.

What to do

Ask the children to wash their hands and put on clean aprons.

Let an adult open the apricots and tip them into the bowl. Supply the children with a plate, knife and fork each and share the apricots among them. Ask them to chop them up, mash them and tip them back into the bowl with the juice.

Add the yoghurt and milk and have the children whisk the mixture before an adult pours it into a blender or food processor to blend for a minute or two.

Pour out the milkshake for the children and suggest they sprinkle a few cornflakes on top for decoration.

Discussion

Encourage children to use size related language, for example, a 'big' jug and 'small' beakers. Pour different quantities of milkshake into two beakers and discuss which one has the most or least, and how to make them both the same.

Follow-up activities

- Give children a copy of the photocopiable sheet 'Apricot milkshakes' on page 71 mounted on card. Discuss each picture and relate it to making the milkshake. Ask the children to cut out the pictures and arrange them in sequence.
- Colour some water with food colouring and corn flour and supply lots of jugs and beakers so that children can explore quantity and capacity as they make pretend milkshakes in a water tray.
- Use the 'Healthy meal' activity on the CD-ROM to provide a link between this activity and the 'Eat more fruit' activity on page 66.

Differentiation

Support younger or less able children by demonstrating how to use tools and equipment. Ask more able children to count the apricot halves in the tin and then calculate how many whole apricots this would be.

ON THE CD-ROM
- On-screen activity 'Healthy meal'
- Photocopiable sheet 'Apricot milkshakes'

Apricot milkshakes

Sound

themes for early years

Go to sleep

What you need

Large open space.

What to do

Ask the children to consider when periods of silence occur in songs and music, for example, at the beginning, at the end and between verses. Introduce the children to the following song, sung to the tune 'Have you seen the Muffin Man?':

'I am going to nod my head, nod my head, nod my head.
But I'm feeling rather tired so now I'll go to sleep.'

Divide the children into two groups and ask one group to sing the song while the other group mimes the actions.

Leave a silent pause after the song and give a signal, such as raising a hand, for the singers to repeat the song. Emphasise the need for those who are miming to remain very still and quiet during the silent period.

Repeat the song three or four times so children can experience both miming and singing.

Alter the words and actions, for example, replace 'nod my head' with 'shake my hands', 'hop up and down' or 'skip around'.

Invite the children to make up their own words and actions.

Discussion

Ask the children to assess how well they managed to maintain the periods of silence. Did it get easier with practice? Why do they think there are silent breaks in songs? Discuss the words of the song, relating them to the body's need for sleep. What happens if we have too little sleep? Compare the times that different children go to bed.

Follow-up activities
- Ask the children to paint pictures of themselves asleep in bed and to record the time when they go to bed.
- Play the song 'Jump for joy' on page 84, inviting children to jump when they hear music and hold a pose during silences.

Differentiation

Ask younger or less able children to sing and mime rather than split them into two groups. Invite more able children to accompany favourite songs with percussion instruments, emphasising the need to hold their instruments very still during any silences.

ON THE CD-ROM
- Song 'Jump for joy'

Small-world play

themes for early years

Road safety

What you need
Play mat with a village or town map marked on it; small world vehicles and characters.

What to do
Invite the children to sit around the mat and take turns to point to features such as roads, houses, a river or a railway line. Ask the children to name landmarks, such as a garage, shop and park. Invite each child to choose a small world character and vehicle and put them in appropriate places on the map.

Challenge the children to find a safe place for their characters to cross the road and discuss appropriate crossing procedures with them.

Ask questions to encourage children to consider appropriate routes, for example, 'Show me how your character would get from the shop to the park'.

Allow time for free play with the resources.

Discussion
Explain that the mat is a simple type of map. Talk about the way that some colours are used to represent things, such as green for grass and blue for water. Talk about the safe places to walk and play. Emphasise the importance of not playing near traffic. Ask the children to suggest other safe crossing places not shown on the map, such as traffic lights, a pelican crossing, a footbridge or an underpass.

> ### Follow-up activities
> - Watch the film clip on the CD-ROM and discuss the safety procedures the children are following.
> - Sing the song 'Stop by the road' on page 85, or listen to it on the CD-ROM, to stimulate further discussion.

Differentiation
Play with younger or less able children to help them to make links between the features on the map and familiar local features within their own experiences. Challenge more able children to make their own maps by drawing on large sheets of paper. Have they included safe places to walk, play and cross the road?

STEPPING STONE
Comment and ask questions about where they live and the natural world.

EARLY LEARNING GOAL
Observe, find out about and identify features in the place they live and the natural world. (KUW)

ASSESSMENT
Observe how the children play to ascertain their awareness of links between map representations and actual features of the locality.

ON THE CD-ROM
- Film clip of children crossing the road
- Song 'Stop by the road'

ICT

STEPPING STONE
Show curiosity about numbers by offering comments or asking questions.

EARLY LEARNING GOAL
Say and use number names in order in familiar contexts. (MD)

ASSESSMENT
Listen to the language used to ascertain whether children are using ordinal language correctly.

Time lines

What you need
Large sheet of white paper; digital camera; printer; string; large coloured bead; brightly coloured backing paper; felt-tipped pens; card.

What to do
Invite the children to make a list of your daily routines on a large sheet of paper, for example, 'arrival', 'registration', 'circle time', 'snack'.

Discuss the order of the routines and explain that some routines, such as registration, happen around the same time each day. Suggest making a 'time line' so that visitors can follow the sequence of your routines.

Take a photograph of each routine throughout the session and print these off. Back a display board with coloured paper and arrange the photographs in time order along the bottom edge. Add captions dictated by the children.

Tie a length of string from one end of the board to the other, just above the photographs, where the children can reach it, and thread a large bead onto it.

Choose a child to move the bead along to the relevant photograph as each routine is followed during a session.

Discussion
When setting up the time line, ask questions such as 'What comes first?' or 'What is the last thing we do before going home?' to encourage children to use appropriate language.

Follow-up activities
● Fill the display space above the time line with the children's drawings and paintings of their routines.
● Read the rhyme 'Daily routines' on page 95 and invite the children to swing a hand backwards and forwards like a pendulum in time to the words 'tick-tock'. Do the children have the same routines? Do they follow the same order?
● Make a 'Daily routines' display, see page 78.

Differentiation
Put routine related objects, such as a beaker or name card, along a shelf at appropriate places under the display so that younger or less able children can make links between real objects and representational items such as photographs. Invite more able children to use a clock face printer to print clocks so that they can draw the time and attach them above the appropriate photograph on the time line.

ON THE CD-ROM
● Poem 'Daily routines'

Stimulus displays can aid the introduction of many aspects of the Myself project. They provide an interesting starting point for discussion and can lead to investigations into other areas.

Setting up displays

Whenever possible, involve the children in setting up the displays. They can help to make component parts and select appropriate backing paper, fabrics, objects and so on. Allow them to experiment with different arrangements and discuss how effective each is. Always try to make the displays interactive. The children will gain much more from a display if they can contribute their own labels or objects that they are then encouraged to handle and touch freely. Similarly, if a display is the focus for a game or activity, the children are more likely to enjoy and remember the information it conveys.

Body parts

What you need

Display board at child height; large piece of thin coloured card; white paper; paints; paintbrushes; scissors; PVA adhesive; paper-clips; small pieces of white card; Stanley knife; felt-tipped pens.

What to do

Invite a child to paint a large simple picture of a child on the white paper, including as many different body parts as possible. When the painting is dry, cut it out and stick it on to the large piece of card. On the small pieces of white card, write labels for the body parts on the painting. Arrange the labels on the card around the picture so that they are near to the corresponding body parts. Cut a slit above each label with the Stanley knife and use a paper-clip to hold the label in position.

Use this display in conjunction with the 'My body' activity described on page 10. Individuals can use a giant cardboard hand to point to the relevant parts of the body as the song is sung.

DISCUSSION

Carry out activities to familiarise the children with the picture and words. Ask a child to point to the label for a specific body part. Alternatively, point to a label and ask a child to read it. Use the detachable labels for matching games. Remove some, or all, of the labels and place them face down on a table. Ask individuals to choose a label and match it to the correct body part. Encourage observation skills by turning some of the labels on the display upside down, removing some or swapping some round. Can the children say what is wrong with the picture and arrange the labels correctly?

Shoe prints

What you need

Display board covered in dark blue backing paper; strips of pale blue sugar paper; blue paint; shallow tray; white paper; two cardboard boxes (one large and one small); blue fabric; collection of shoes (only one shoe from each pair); scissors, felt-tipped pens; glue sticks; stapler.

What to do

Invite one or two children to help make the border by printing blue footprints with the paint on to the strips of pale blue sugar paper. To obtain good prints, make sure that the children's feet are evenly covered with paint and that they place their feet flat on to the paper. When dry, glue the border strips around the edge of the display board.

On the white paper, draw round a shoe twice, then cut out these outlines and use them as labels for the display. Write 'Shoe prints' on the labels and staple them in place near the top of the display.

Use the blue paint to take a print from the sole of each of the shoes on the white paper. When dry, cut out the shoe print and glue it to the display board.

Write a label 'Match the shoes to the prints' and staple it in place at the bottom of the display.

Place the cardboard boxes together on one side of the display board. Drape the boxes with the blue fabric and arrange the shoes on the boxes so that the children have easy access both to the shoes and to the prints. Link this display to the 'Shoe mimes' activity on page 25.

DISCUSSION

Invite the children to look carefully at the sole of each shoe and to find the corresponding print on the display board. Encourage them to consider the size, shape and pattern on each sole. Also use the display to stimulate discussion about footwear. Why do we wear shoes? Examine each shoe in detail. Who would wear it and when? Describe the size, shape, colour and materials used. What type of fastening does it have? Why do some shoes have a deep tread on the sole, while others have none?

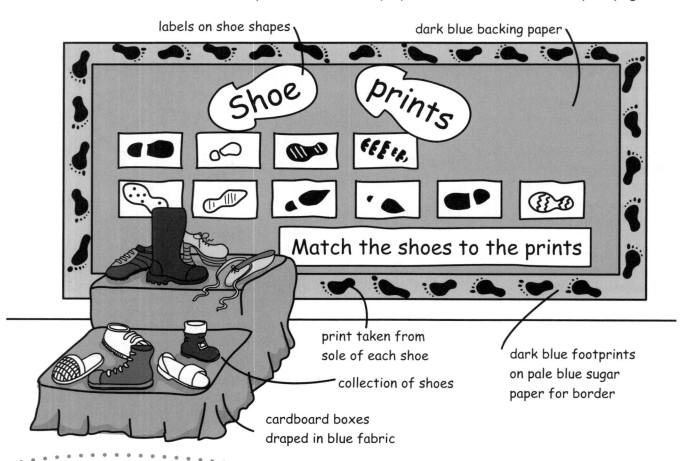

labels on shoe shapes

dark blue backing paper

Shoe prints

Match the shoes to the prints

print taken from sole of each shoe

collection of shoes

dark blue footprints on pale blue sugar paper for border

cardboard boxes draped in blue fabric

Action words

What you need
Display board covered in black backing paper; white paper; scissors; felt-tipped pens; sticky tape; stapler; drawing pins; card; camera.

What to do
Take photographs of the children involved in various activities, for example, playing with sand, building with construction toys, painting, reading or doing some physical activity on a climbing frame.

Fix the photographs to the display board with a curl of sticky tape at the back. Write the question 'What can you do?' on to a card label and staple it in place at the top of the display board.

Make some concertina people using the white paper. Fold them as for a zigzag book, draw a large simple outline of a child on the front section and cut it out, leaving the hands attached at the paper's edge to act as a hinge.

Repeat this so you have several strings of people. Use a drawing pin to fix each concertina of people (folded up) on to the display board amongst the photographs. Link this display to the 'What I can do' activity on page 48.

DISCUSSION
Allow the children a period of time to study the photographs individually and then gather them around the display. Talk about the photographs, identifying the children in them and the activities they are doing. Explain that you want the children to think of as many 'action' words as possible to describe the activities in the photographs. Record each action word by writing it on to one of the concertina people, for example, the children may suggest 'jumping', 'sliding', 'painting', 'splashing' and 'building'. Unfold one of the concertina people for each new word. Have some extra blank concertina people available, so that the children can continue to add new action words over the next few days. Encourage them to count the number of words they have thought of. What do they notice about the end of each word?

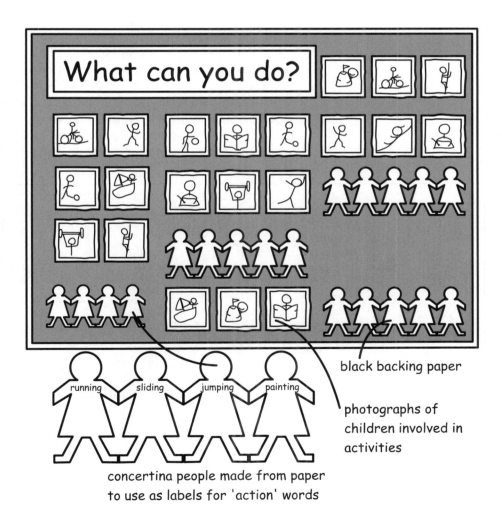

black backing paper

photographs of children involved in activities

concertina people made from paper to use as labels for 'action' words

running   sliding   jumping   painting

Daily routines

DISCUSSION
Encourage the children to handle and play freely with the items on display and to return them to the appropriate surfaces afterwards. Join children as they play to encourage them to talk about their own daily routines.

What you need
Display board covered in bright backing paper in contrasting dark and light colours; white paper and card; felt-tipped pens; scissors; glue; mark-making materials; mail order catalogues; six cardboard boxes, three matching pairs of different heights; colourful fabric; objects related to the routines of dressing, washing, cleaning teeth, eating, playing and sleeping; photographs of the children supplied by parents; stapler.

What to do
Explain to parents beforehand about the subject of the display and ask them to take photographs of their children involved in daily routines such as washing and dressing.

Create a border for the display board from a contrasting colour. Entitle the display 'Daily routines'. Make six different mathematical shapes, such as a triangle and square, from card and mount each one on dark backing paper. Label each shape with a different routine: 'dressing', 'washing', 'cleaning teeth', 'eating', 'playing' and 'sleeping'.

Invite the children to look in catalogues for pictures of routines, for example, a child in nightclothes climbing into a bed, and store them in six separate containers, one for each of the routines depicted. Stick the pictures and appropriate small objects chosen by the children onto each shape. Staple the finished shapes to the large display. Arrange the cardboard boxes in height order at either side of the display and drape them in fabric to create six separate surfaces.

Create card 'Daily routine' labels for each surface to match those on the display. Invite the children to arrange suitable objects associated with each routine beside each label. Make links between the display and the daily routine time line on page 74. Suggest making a time line of children's home routines using the display as a stimulus for ideas. Say the rhyme 'Daily routines' on page 95 or listen to it on the CD-ROM, and make links between the routines mentioned, those on the display and the children's comments about their personal routines.

each shape has small pictures from magazines, and small objects taped on

objects on each surface relate to the corresponding routine

I'm alive shanty

Here's my head, my think-ing head; I'm a-live to-day! My think-ing brain's in-side my head. I'm a-live to-day!

Chorus
I'm a-live, we're a-live, We laugh and sing and play.
I'm a-live, we're a-live, so let's en-joy the day.

2. Here's my eyes, my seeing eyes;
I see the world through my eyes.

Chorus

3. Here's my mouth, my speaking mouth;
I talk and sing with my mouth.

Chorus

4. Here's my nose, my smelling nose;
I smell the world with my nose.

Chorus

5. Here am I, all of me;
And that's the way I want to be.

Chorus

Ian Henderson-Begg

With my hands

I can fas - ten my coat,
fas - ten my co at, fas ten my coat. I can
fas - ten my coat, With my hands.

v.2 I can wash my face

v.3 I can eat my lunch

v.4 I can play with my toys

v.5 I can hold a cup

v.6 I can stroke the dog

Sally Scott

That hat!

*This will change according to the type of hat.

**Child does actions, for example, climb the rigging, coil the rope and so on.

Additional verses on CD-ROM

Peter Morrell

Shoe choose tune

2. If I could choose what shoes to have,
   Some dancing shoes I'd wear.
   Tip-tap here. Tip-tap there. etc

3. If I could choose what shoes to have,
   Some flip-flop shoes I'd wear.
   Flip-flop here. Flip-flop there. etc.

4. If I could choose what shoes to have,
   Some horse's shoes I'd wear.
   Clip-clop here. Clip-clop there. etc.

5. If I could choose what shoes to have,
   Some slippers I would wear.
   Creep, creep here. Creep, creep there. etc.

Clive and Thomas Barnwell

All about me

I have got two legs to run to my friends,
Run to my friends, run to my friends.
I have got two legs to run to my friends,
And I have got two feet and knees to bend

I have got two eyes to look at my friends,
Look at my friends, look at my friends.
I have got two eyes to look at my friends,
And I have got two feet and knees to bend.

I have got two ears to listen to my friends,
Listen to my friends, listen to my friends.
I have got two ears to listen to my friends,
And I have got two feet and knees to bend.

I have got one mouth to smile at my friends,
Smile at my friends, smile at my friends.
I have got one mouth to smile at my friends,
And I have got two feet and knees to bend.

I have got two arms to cuddle my friends,
Cuddle my friends, cuddle my friends.
I have got two arms to cuddle my friends,
And I have got two feet and knees to bend.

Sally Scott

Pets

Claire has got a cat, it is fluffy as can be.
Molly is her name and she is lovely.

Chorus
Who has got a pet? Come tell us all today.
Tell us about your pet, tell us all today.

Aidan has a fish, it is scaly as can be.
Goldy is her name and she is lovely.

Who has got a pet come tell us all today.
Tell us about your pet, tell us all today.

Vikram has a dog, it is hairy as can be.
Dougal is his name and he is lovely.

Patrick has a snail, it is slimy as can be.
Steven is his name and he is lovely.

Yuriko has a mouse, it is tiny as can be.
Florence is her name and she is lovely.

Sally Scott

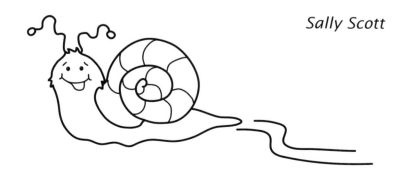

Visitors

My best friend came on Monday, he came
to visit me.
We played with some toys, we made lots of
noise.
He came to visit me.

The doctor came on Tuesday, she came to
visit me.
She looked at my head, and sent me to
bed.
She came to visit me.

The postman came on Wednesday, he came
to visit me.
He knocked on the door, a parcel I saw.
He came to visit me.

My neighbour came on Thursday, she came
to visit me.
We had a good chat, about this and that.
She came to visit me.

A hedgehog came on Friday, it came to
visit me.
It rolled in a ball, it curled tight and small,
It came to visit me.

A painter came on Saturday, he came to
visit me,
He painted the hall, and the garden wall.
He came to visit me.

Sally Scott

Jump for joy

When it's nice and su - nny, I jump for joy.

I jump for joy, I jump for joy. When it's nice and su - nny,

I jump for joy, I jump for joy, yes I jump for joy.

When it's time for Christmas, I jump for joy,
I jump for joy, I jump for joy.
When it's time for Christmas, I jump for joy,
I jump for joy, yes I jump for joy.

When it is my birthday, I jump for joy,
I jump for joy, I jump for joy.
When it is my birthday, I jump for joy,
I jump for joy, yes I jump for joy.

When it is Diwali, I jump for joy,
I jump for joy, I jump for joy.
When it is S, I jump for joy,
I jump for joy, yes I jump for joy.

When we're at the seaside, I jump for joy,
I jump for joy, I jump for joy.
When we're at the seaside I jump for joy!
I jump for joy, yes I jump for joy.

Sally Scott

Stop by the road

Please take someone's hand.
Please take someone's hand.
To cross the road safely,
Please take someone's hand.

Please listen out for cars.
Please listen out for cars.
To cross the road safely,
Please listen out for cars.

Please look both ways.
Please look both ways.
To cross the road safely,
Please look both ways.

Only when it's safe,
Only when it's safe,
Please cross the road safely,
Only when it's safe.

Sally Scott

This day is a special day

Jenny is 3 years today.
Let's all sing 'Hip hip hooray!'.
This day is a special day,
For it is Jenny's birthday.

This day is a special day.
Let's all sing 'Hip hip hooray!'.
This day is a special day,
For it is Omar's birthday.

Omar is 4 years today.
Let's all sing 'Hip hip hooray!'.
This day is a special day,
For it is Omar's birthday.

Sally Scott

Tommy Thumb

Tommy Thumb, Tommy Thumb, where are you?
Here I am, here I am,
How do you do?
Peter Pointer, Peter Pointer, where are you?
Here I am, here I am,
How do you do?
Middleman Tall, Middleman Tall, where are you?
Here I am, here I am,
How do you do?
Ruby Ring, Ruby Ring, where are you?
Here I am, here I am,
How do you do?
Baby Small, Baby Small, where are you?
Here I am, here I am,
How do you do?

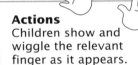

Actions
Children show and
wiggle the relevant
finger as it appears.

Quiet as mice

Quick –
be quiet as mice.
Don't make a sound.
Shhhh.

Quick – sit.

Upon the ground
without a sound!

Quick – stand.

Hold out your hand
without a sound.

Quick – hop.

To the baker's shop
without a sound.

Quick – skip.

Don't slippety slip
without a sound.

Pie Corbett

I can

I can count to ten,
Touch my toes,
Fasten buttons
And tie bows.

I can clean my teeth,
Wash my face,
Brush my hair
Into place.

I can stand up straight,
See how tall!
Or curl up tight
Round and small.

I can walk quickly
Or stand still,
Pretend to climb
Up the hill.

I can run and leap,
Skip and hop.
I can climb up
To the top.

I can taste and touch,
Hear and smell.
What a lot I
Can do well!

Tomorrow I'll try
Something new.
Change 'I can't' to
'I can do!'

Rozalia Makinson

Animal sounds we can make

After we count three
show us who
you can be –
one, two, three –

ROAR – like a lion prowling.

GRRRRR – like a tiger growling.

PURR – like a sleepy cat.

SQUEAK – like a flying bat.

BARK – like an angry dog.

CROAK – like a funny frog.

Pie Corbett

Bedtime in summer

In summer, it's light
When I go to bed;
The sun's wide awake
As I bury my head
Between the sheets,
So crisp and white,
And try to sleep
Sweet dreams all night.

BUT

the puppy next door
Begins to yap
And a branch on my window
Goes 'tip tap tap'.

No wonder the sun
Is shining bright –
It's TOO EARLY FOR BED
On this fine summer's night!

Trevor Harvey

That's my face

That's my face,
Look can you see?
Here are my eyes,
They are part of me.

That's my face,
Look can you see?
Here is my nose,
It is part of me.

That's my face,
Look can you see?
Here are my ears,
They are part of me.

That's my face,
Look can you see?
Here is my mouth,
It is part of me.

That's my face,
Look can you see?
Here are my teeth,
They are part of me.

Sally Scott

Actions
Invite children to point to each facial feature, then put their hands on their chests as they say 'part of me'.

Dressing up

What is in the dressing up box?
Hats and coats and shoes and socks!
A fairy princess, I want to be
I'll find a long dress, Now look at me!

What is in the dressing up box?
Hats and coats and shoes and socks!
A handsome prince, I want to be
I'll find a gold crown, Now look at me!

What is in the dressing up box?
Hats and coats and shoes and socks!
A magic wizard, I want to be
I'll find a big cloak, Now look at me!

What is in the dressing up box?
Hats and coats and shoes and socks!
A friendly witch, I want to be
I'll find a broomstick, Now look at me

Sally Scott

Once I was a baby

Once I was a baby, I was very, very small,
I couldn't do anything, anything at all.
I couldn't even walk and I couldn't even talk,
Once I was a baby, I was very, very small.

Once I was a baby, I was very, very small,
I couldn't do anything, anything at all.
I cried quite a lot and I slept in a cot,
Once I was a baby, I was very, very small.

Once I was a baby, I was very, very small,
I couldn't do anything, anything at all.
I couldn't put on clothes and I couldn't blow my nose,
Once I was a baby, I was very, very small.

Once I was a baby, I was very, very small,
I couldn't do anything, anything at all.
I couldn't say my name and I couldn't play a game,
Once I was a baby, I was very, very small.

Sally Scott

My worries

My worry was a nasty pain,
Right inside my tummy,
It really wouldn't go away,
And so I told my mummy.

My worry was the darkness,
And shadows on the wall,
Making scary monster shapes,
So I told my brother Paul.

My worry was my sister,
Because she looked so sad,
I couldn't make her smile at me,
And so I told my Dad.

My worry was fat spiders,
Hiding beside my bed,
Ready to jump and frighten me,
So I told my Grandpa Ted.

I always share my worries,
With my family every day,
Then they don't come back again,
They simply go away!

Sally Scott

Clapping clothes

My hat has just one clap, just one clap for me,
My hat has just one clap, sound one clap for me.
HAT!
Children clap once while saying 'hat'.

My jumper has two claps, two claps for me,
My jumper has two claps, sound two claps for me.
JUM-PER!
Children clap twice while saying 'jumper'.

My cardigan has three claps, three claps for me,
My cardigan has three claps, sound three claps for me.
CAR-DI-GAN!
Children clap three times while saying 'cardigan'

My Wellington boots have four claps, four claps for me,
My Wellington boots have four claps, sound four claps for
me.
WELL-ING-TON BOOTS!
Children clap four times while saying 'Wellington boots'

Sally Scott

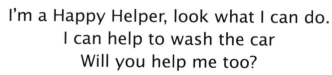

Happy helpers

I'm a Happy Helper, look what I can do.
I can help to sweep the floor.
Will you help me too?

I'm a Happy Helper, look what I can do.
I can help to tidy up.
Will you help me too?

I'm a Happy Helper, look what I can do.
I can help to wipe the table.
Will you help me too?

I'm a Happy Helper, look what I can do.
I can help to wash the car
Will you help me too?

Sally Scott

Hand washing

Wash, wash my hands, every day
To make sure I wash all the germs right away.
When I go to the toilet I remember to say
Wash, wash my hands 'til the germs go away.

Wash, wash my hands, every day
To make sure I wash all the germs right away.
When I've eaten some food I remember to say
Wash, wash my hands 'til the germs go away.

Wash, wash my hands, every day
To make sure I wash all the germs right away.
When I've played outside I remember to say
Wash, wash my hands 'til the germs go away.

Wash, wash my hands, every day
To make sure I wash all the germs right away.
When I've tidied the room I remember to say
Wash, wash my hands 'til the germs go away.

Sally Scott

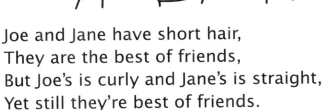

Best of friends

Joe and Jane live next door,
They are the best of friends,
But Joe likes chips and Jane likes mash,
Yet still they're best of friends.

Joe and Jane both ride bikes,
They are the best of friends,
But Joe's is red and Jane's is blue,
Yet still they're best of friends.

Joe and Jane have short hair,
They are the best of friends,
But Joe's is curly and Jane's is straight,
Yet still they're best of friends.

Joe and Jane climb tall trees,
They are the best of friends,
But Joe stays low and Jane goes high,
Yet still they're best of friends.

Sally Scott

Patterns in socks

Look at all the different socks,
On the washing line,
Sarah's socks are short and pink,
But they are not like mine.

Look at all the different socks,
On the washing line,
India's socks are stripy and green,
But they are not like mine.

Look at all the different socks,
On the washing line,
Grandad's socks are long and grey,
But they are not like mine.

Look at all the different socks,
On the washing line,
Connor's socks are red and blue,
But they are not like mine.

Look at all the different socks,
On the washing line,
My favourite socks have spots and stars,
AND THAT'S BECAUSE THEY'RE MINE!

Sally Scott

Happy news, sad news

Children, children, tell your news,
Before we go and play,
What have you been doing?
Come, make us smile today.

Sam has a sister, tiny and new,
Eimear can ride her bike,
Miah's puppy has started to chew,
Simon went for a hike.

Children, children, tell your news,
Before we go and play,
What have you been doing?
Come, share your sadness today.

Sam's little sister was crying,
Eimear fell off her bike,
Miah's puppy chewed her shoes,
Simon got lost on his hike.

Children you have told your news,
What tales you had to tell,
You made us smile with happy talk,
And we've shared your sadness as well.

Sally Scott

Myself

Daily routines

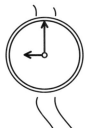

At 9 o'clock, tick, tock.
Come inside, tick, tock.
At 9 o'clock, tick, tock.
Tick, tock, tick, tock.

At 10 o'clock, tick, tock.
Have a snack, tick, tock.
At 10 o'clock, tick, tock.
Tick, tock, tick, tock.

At 11 o'clock, tick, tock
Play outside, tick, tock
At 11 o'clock, tick, tock
Tick, tock, tick, tock.

At 12 o'clock, tick, tock
Have some lunch, tick, tock
At 12 o'clock, tick, tock
Tick, tock, tick, tock.

At 1 o'clock, tick, tock
Look at books, tick, tock
At 1 o'clock, tick, tock
Tick, tock, tick, tock.

At 2 o'clock, tick, tock
Time to paint, tick, tock
At 2 o'clock, tick, tock
Tick, tock, tick, tock.

At 3 o'clock, tick, tock
Dance and sing, tick, tock
At 3 o'clock, tick, tock
Tick, tock, tick, tock.

At 4 o'clock, tick, tock
Say goodbye, tick, tock
At 4 o'clock, tick, tock
Tick, tock, tick, tock.
Sally Scott

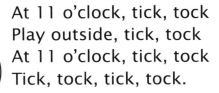
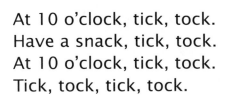
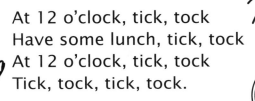
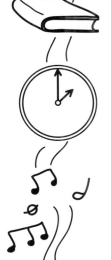

Keeping safe

Knives are dangerous,
They are not for me,
Knives are sharp,
And they will cut me.

Matches are dangerous,
They are not for me,
Matches make fire,
And they will burn me.

Scissors are dangerous,
They are not for me,
Scissors are sharp,
And they will cut me.

Plugs are dangerous,
They are not for me,
Plugs are electric,
And they might hurt me.

Kettles are dangerous,
They are not for me,
Kettles are boiling hot,
And they will burn me.

Sally Scott

In this series:

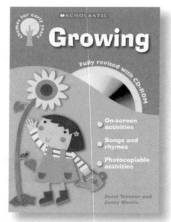

ISBN 0-439-96559-4
ISBN 978-0439-96559-0

ISBN 0-439-96558-6
ISBN 978-0439-96558-3

ISBN 0-439-96560-8
ISBN 978-0439-96560-6

ISBN 0-439-96557-8
ISBN 978-0439-96557-6

To find out more about **Themes for Early Years** or to order additional copies of the CD-ROMs call **0845 603 9091**

**New Themes for Early Years - available Spring 2007
Minibeasts ISBN 0-439-94497-X
People who help us ISBN 0-439-94498-8**

Visit our website **www.scholastic.co.uk**